Edwin Smith
A Life in Derbyshire Cricket

Steve Dolman

Dedication

To Mum and Dad. Thank you for all your early support and
encouragement that fostered a lifelong love of Derbyshire cricket.
Hopefully all those trips in the Ford Anglia were worth it ...

First published in Great Britain by
Association of Cricket Statisticians and Historians
Cardiff CF11 9XR.
© ACS, 2015

British Library Cataloguing-in-Publication Data.
A catalogue record for this book is available from the British Library.

ISBN: 978 1 908165 61 9
Typeset and printed by The City Press Leeds Ltd

Contents

Introduction

Edwin Smith is a Derbyshire legend. It is not a status that one acquires easily in life; in Edwin's case, it was down to bowling over 13,000 overs for the county, over a career that ran from 1951 to 1971.

Only seven men have taken 1,000 career wickets for the club and Edwin was the last to reach that milestone. In all likelihood he will be the last, given the limitation on County Championship cricket today and the greater mobility of players, keen to make the most from a relatively short career.

He took a hundred wickets in a season once, in 1955, but spinners rarely do that on Derbyshire wickets and certainly not when you're coming on after the legendary Cliff Gladwin and Les Jackson. Edwin normally got on as second change, after Derek Morgan and there were many times when there wasn't much left by that point.

When the great pair retired, they were replaced by Harold Rhodes and Brian Jackson. More bowlers who often took out the top order and a good part of the middle, leaving Edwin to feast on the scraps that remained. If they failed, it was usually a good batting wicket and his role would often become that of stock bowler, keeping it quiet, but not missing the chance of winkling one out with his off spin variations.

There were certain tracks around the county circuit where spin was the road to success, and that is where he was expected to cash in – and usually did. He took five wickets in an innings on 51 occasions and year after year took between 60 and 90 wickets, ending his career with 1217 of them at less than 26 runs each. As for the economy rate, he went for less than two-and-a-half runs an over, the benchmark of parsimony by which the very best Derbyshire bowlers have been judged.

I saw Edwin bowl on many occasions, but wish I could turn the clock back and see him again with the benefit of experience. I was 12 when he retired and in the naivety of youth was more taken by the pace of Alan Ward and Harold Rhodes, little realising the consummate guile that made Edwin one of the best bowlers of his type in the country, this at a time when there were a lot more of them to admire than there are today.

If he was playing now he would walk into the England team, as a cunning bowler who imparted strong spin between his index and middle fingers. He was a master of flight, line and length and when you're considering the greatest Derbyshire spinners, then he has to be included in the discussions. It is tribute to his skill that, when we signed the great Indian spinner Srinivasan Venkataraghavan in the mid-1970s, my father watched the new overseas signing for a few overs then shook his head.

'He's all right,' he said, 'but he's no Edwin Smith.' Praise indeed.

He could bat, too and often fought bravely in a rearguard action. He latterly got between five and seven hundred runs a summer, had a safe pair of hands and ended up as county coach for several seasons. A man of parts, for sure.

He is also thoroughly engaging company. He has a ready and regular laugh and a remarkable recall for the players and events of the past, with an extraordinary collection of memorabilia from his long career. In the hours that I spent with him and his delightful wife Jean, he was patient and accommodating, always willing to tell me more as I sought the answers to questions that had in some cases been in my head for years.

He was one of the county's finest – and this is his story.

Chapter One
Early days

The long-established village of Grassmoor is three miles to the south of Chesterfield, in north-east Derbyshire. Sixteenth century parish records refer to it as Gresmore and perhaps its best-known resident was the former butler to Princess Diana, Paul Burrell, who grew up in the village. But that is only if you are not a cricket fan.

Like so many villages throughout Nottinghamshire and Derbyshire, it was for many years home to coal miners and in its heyday around 90 per cent of the male population worked at the colliery. In the early 19th century, there was evidence that rich seams of coal lay in the ground beneath the village and a number of entrepreneurs and industrialists made preliminary investigations into the viability of its extraction. One such businessman, Alfred Barnes, took the plunge to excavate the first mine shaft at Grassmoor, and got a team of miners working on it. They found rich seams of coal, and a colliery was built and fitted out with the necessary equipment, officially opening in 1880.

Accommodation was built for the colliery workers and their families in two rows of terraced houses. One of these rows was called East Street, just a short walk from the colliery, but the locals called it 'Sluggards Row'. The miners living in East Street tended to be the ones who arrived at work last and so a name was born.

The second row was named Grasshill Street. These houses were built in the late 19th century, on a site that was a little further away from the colliery than East Street. It was more commonly the home of colliery officials and was nicknamed 'Four Bob Row' because, as the name suggests, the rent for each house was four shillings each week.

The rows provided basic but dry accommodation for the workers and their families and the community grew as the colliery prospered. It was a successful enterprise, regarded as one of the best in the county and made Mr Barnes a very wealthy man. He later became Liberal MP for Chesterfield and also president of the Mining Association of Great Britain.

He died in 1901, but his family were keen to give something back to the people of Grassmoor and invested in the land that later became Barnes Park, which opened in 1920. It originally had fields for playing football and cricket, swings for small children, a bowling green and tennis courts. The last two of these are long since gone, but the others survive and continue to do well.

On 19 November 1933, an explosion occurred at the colliery, caused by

Grassmoor Cricket Club in the 1920s. Edwin's father sitting, extreme right, front row (Grassmoor Cricket Club)

East Street, or Sluggards Row, undated. (North Wingfield History Society)

the ignition of the flammable coal gas, methane. Fourteen men died in the accident, with a further eight seriously injured. Although there had been numerous deaths at the colliery, this was the first major incident, although one with which their counterparts around the country had become all too familiar.

Arthur Bedford Smith was one of the men in this tragedy, but he was one of the lucky ones. He was badly gassed, but recovered and was one of only three miners who returned to the mine afterwards.

He had been at the colliery since the war, when he had narrowly avoided a call to arms. He was in the next scheduled draft when the war ended in 1918 and intead continued to work with the many who toiled long, dark hours underground.

Less than two months after the disaster, on 2 January 1934, he became a father for the fourth time as a son, Edwin, was born to Arthur and his wife Annie (nee Eastwood).

Annie had endured her fair share of heartache. She had married her first husband, Albert Wright, in July 1913 but he had died in Flanders during the Great War, while serving in the Sherwood Foresters. His death is recorded on the Arras Memorial. Annie then married a Grassmoor man, Joe Pickering, in September 1918, but he had died in a fall at the colliery in August 1919, aged only 19. She married Arthur in December, 1920 and one cannot imagine what thoughts had passed through her mind, seven months into pregnancy, at the possibility of losing a third husband.

All turned out well, however and Edwin joined a family that already contained his brother, Arthur and sisters Elsie and Doris. With Annie's two children by Albert Wright, Walter and Gladys, also in the house, money was tight. The new addition to the family was considerably younger, but was doted upon and, while money was scarce, the family environment was a loving one.

From an early age he was known as 'Tat', a nickname that stuck with him throughout his cricket career. The origins of that name are unknown, although his father, grandfather and brother all answered to it in their turn.

There was always a football available and a cricket bat was propped up at the side of the door, ready for use when the weather was at all favourable. The youngsters enjoyed trips to the local cinema in Grassmoor, where there were two shows a week, one running from Monday to Wednesday, the other from Thursday to Saturday. Edwin especially enjoyed westerns and the films of Roy Rogers and Gene Autry were particular favourites, as, in different vein, were those of Fred Astaire and Ginger Rogers.

The cinema, originally called The Electric, was later renamed The Roxy and was at the far end of the village. It opened in 1936 and in the pre-television era was an escape from everyday life. In its heyday thousands passed through its doors to enjoy the latest Hollywood films, 'enjoying' facilities that were far from sophisticated, but generally being oblivious to them.

There had been an earlier cinema in the village, at the top of New Street, which was later turned into a billiard hall called The Drum. Here, when he reached the minimum age of 14 that was required for entry, the young Edwin spent many hours learning skills that would later turn him into a respected and feared amateur snooker player.

Like the village's other children, Edwin attended Grassmoor Primary School, before progressing to what was locally called 'the big school' when he was eight. His school education from 11, which like so many others ended at 15, was completed at North Wingfield School under the watching eye of the formidable Joseph 'Joby' Harris.

Mr Harris was a 'strict, but fair' head teacher, according to Edwin and importantly for a sports-mad youngster was himself a very good cricketer. He played for Clay Cross, as well as for Grassmoor and is remembered as an important catalyst in a fledgling career. Cricket facilities were limited and games largely took place in the school yard, but Edwin remembers Mr Harris coming out at breaks to teach them rudimentary cricket techniques in favourable weather.

The head teacher was at the helm of the school from the mid-1930s to his retirement in the 1960s, throughout that time providing strong leadership and even stronger discipline. A few may have resented this, but for the majority it ensured that their school days were undertaken in a safe and enjoyable environment.

Many years later, while fielding at fine leg in a match between Derbyshire and Hampshire at Bournemouth in 1964, Edwin was tapped on the shoulder and turned to see his old head teacher for the first time in many years. A later chat revealed that he had retired to the south coast after the death of his wife to live with his daughter and her family.

When asked about his favourite subjects at school, Edwin laughs.

> Cricket and football! I was never much of a student but we played cricket in the yard in the summer months and the rest of the time it was football. I played in the school team and was a right-winger who scored a few goals. I was quite quick and we did fairly well. One year we won the Chesterfield Schools Challenge Shield and there were some good players in that side.

> A couple of the lads went for trials with league clubs later, but there was more money in working down the pit in those days! Another, Ben Stoppard, became a good enough sprinter to run against and come a close second to McDonald Bailey. They raced against each other at Queens Park in Chesterfield, when there was a running track there.

The Trinidad-born Bailey won a bronze medal in the Helsinki Olympic Games of 1952, having earlier finished sixth in the same 100 metres in the 1948 games in London. He was the outstanding sprinter of the generation and in 1951 equalled the then world record of 10.1 seconds. It had stood since 1936 and had been set by the legendary American sprinter Jesse Owens. That a young local lad was good enough to run such an athlete close was indicative of the talent often present in such small communities.

Edwin's football effectively finished when he joined Derbyshire, although he made a few appearances in local football in his mid-20s, while recovering from a leg injury. Such later team mates as Ian Hall, Ian Buxton and Ray Swallow made a name for themselves in both sports, but Edwin modestly admits that he 'wasn't as good as them'.

What were his memories of school yard and street cricket before he joined the village club?

> We used to play as often as we could. There was usually a bat to be had, but we had to use our initiative for balls. We often used 'coconut' balls – the wooden ones that people threw at the coconuts on the fairground. We would cover them with black tape and play until the tape came off and then cover them again.

> Occasionally we got our hands on a cricket ball, but it was usually one that had been deemed unfit for use at the cricket club. If you were lucky there would still be some leather on it and we would again tape it up, but sometimes there was just the string covering the ball and the tape would come out again. We also used the old composition balls, or 'compos' as we called them. I broke a few windows hitting them over the years!

A move to a bigger house at 20 Birkin Lane in 1942, when he was eight, exposed young Edwin to organised cricket. The house was across the road from the cricket ground, which provided the ideal playground for a sports-mad youngster. The road was swapped for the outfield as he and his friends spent many happy hours there. A typically boyish thing caused a setback when he contracted pneumonia, a potentially fatal illness that was more dangerous at that time before antibiotics.

> I'd been rolling around in wet grass and I suppose the houses themselves were fairly damp too, so I didn't get dried off, or change my clothes. I was seriously ill for weeks and at one stage the local doctor and nurse spent a couple of nights with me, because they were concerned that I wouldn't pull through. I spent weeks in my bedroom and missed quite a lot of school as a result.

This was in wartime, when Chesterfield and district got away quite lightly in comparison to other areas. The German air force tried to bomb the Horns Bridge at Chesterfield, which carried three railway lines up, down and across the country, but they failed because the town kept an impressively strict blackout. Near to the bridge was the Chesterfield Tube Works, which produced shell casings and barrels for guns, mortars and other wartime components, so damage to either could have impaired the British war effort.

A few bombs were dropped in the area around Grassmoor, but these were largely 'ditched' by aircraft returning to Germany after bombing elsewhere, the larger industrial areas of Sheffield and Derby bearing the brunt.

For the local school children, life went on largely as it had done before. Food and commodities were in short supply but the resourcefulness of families ensured that meals were fashioned from the most basic of ingredients and that nothing was wasted. This continued for many years afterwards, rationing only ending in July 1954.

By the summer of 1949, Edwin had started to attend cricket nets at Grassmoor Cricket Club. At 15, he was fleet-footed and sure-handed in the field and had impressed people in the nets with a natural and easy action that changed little throughout his long career.

His family had played a major part in the history of the club, which dates from 1884. His grandfather, Arthur Bedford, had been a founder member and took seven wickets in the club's first recorded game. A left-arm medium pace bowler, he made more money playing for local sides than he did working at the colliery. He once won the 'All England Amateur Bowling Prize', of two classic books with brass clasps. He continued to take wickets for years afterwards and earned himself a considerable reputation.

Edwin's father was himself a useful cricketer, being remembered as a good left-handed round-arm swing bowler who could score handy runs down the order. Meanwhile, Edwin's elder brother, also named Arthur, became a mainstay of the club for decades. Making his debut in 1935, he played for Grassmoor until 1978 and made thousands of runs, as well as taking hundreds of wickets with a mixture of leg spin, top spin and off spin.

He lost crucial years to the war but had a successful spell at Saltaire in the Bradford League. He then spent a short time on the county staff, making an appearance for Derbyshire as a substitute fielder in July 1947, against Kent, at Abbeydale Park in Sheffield, before the re-drawing of county boundaries made this a Yorkshire ground. Arthur's contribution was catching the Kent opening batsman Leslie Todd from the bowling of a new young county bowler by the name of Les Jackson. It was quite a claim to fame, being involved in the first county wicket taken by a man who would go on to be regarded as the county's greatest-ever bowler.

Edwin in short had much to live up to as he made his Grassmoor debut for the second team.

He performed steadily, if in unspectacular fashion, but it was as the balmy summer days turned cooler and the season entered its closing weeks that events conspired to change the course of his life. Grassmoor second eleven was lacking players by the last three games of the season and bowlers, in particular, were in short supply. The skipper, Wilf Hawkins, asked Edwin if he would like to bowl and was met with a trademark grin. Let him take up the story:

> I marked out a run to bowl medium pace and started to set a field, but Wilf told me "No – you are going to bowl off spin, like you do in the nets."

> So I did. In that first match I took four for none against Dronfield, then the following week I took five for 37 at Whittington. The last game of

the season was against Chesterfield Tube Works and they were top of the league. I remember we were a few players short and my brother, Arthur, dropped down to play for us so we could get something close to a team.

I took six for 13 and we bowled them out for 37. After that I was seen primarily as a bowler and everything developed fairly quickly from there.

Within two summers, at the age of 17, he was in the county first eleven.

North Wingfield School football team, 1947-48 – Back row, left to right:
Jobey Harris, Graham Winn, Derek Jones, Lol Taylor, Jack Mellors,
Lenny Winn, Norman Millington, 'Rab' Turnbull.
Centre: Edwin Smith, Alan North, Jesse Fletcher, 'Kidder' Beeson, Jeff Mann.
Front: Frank Rough, Colin Thackray. (unknown)

Chapter Two

The young cricketer

Edwin's good performances in the early season of 1950 earned him an opportunity in the Grassmoor first eleven. 'I had to be good,' said Edwin, 'because my uncle was the first team off spinner and I took his place.' His strong performances continued in the senior side, a stand out being against Clay Cross and Danesmoor Miners Welfare, when the opposition had reached 49 for one in reply to Grassmoor's 61 all out.

At that point, Edwin was introduced, somewhat belatedly, into the attack and proved unplayable. He took seven wickets for one run in 17 balls, as Clay Cross crashed to 51 all out.

Four successive matches brought him 25 wickets for just 59 runs and to the attention of Derbyshire's secretary Will Taylor, who offered him a game against Yorkshire under-17s at Chesterfield. Harry Elliott, the county coach, had previously spotted Edwin's talent in a coaching session at Clay Cross and the invitation was duly issued.

> Yorkshire had a strong side. Doug Padgett, Ray Illingworth, Ken Taylor and Bryan Stott, all of them to become county stalwarts, were in the opposition and we were hammered. They won by nine wickets, after we made less than 80. I did pretty well, though and my figures were ten overs for 11 runs and the one wicket that fell. It made an impression and I was offered a one-month trial in 1951.

How did the money compare with what he was earning at Grassmoor Colliery? By this time, Edwin was working as a mechanic down the pit and following in the family footsteps.

> I was offered that trial in Derby at six pounds a week. I remember going down there with my father on the train and when we got to the ground, we said our farewells and he told me: 'You're on your own now, son.'

> I was in digs at a guest house run by Mrs Silkstone on Babington Lane in Derby and they cost me two pound and five shillings a week. After two weeks there I decided I would travel back and forward each day, which cost me 30 shillings [£1.50 today]. It didn't leave me an awful lot of money for socialising or for anything else really, but it was down to me to make the best of it.

> I felt very lonely and alone that first night, but things improved as I started to get to know a few people and started playing cricket.

Harry Elliott, the club's coach and long-time wicket-keeper, thought there was something about the slight youngster. He got good spin from a grip that came naturally to him, while he had the natural and precious gift of flight, this following a short, skipping run of six paces that took little out of him and meant he could bowl long spells. While the succession of seam bowlers in the county was known to cricket fans across of the country, Derbyshire had more recently enjoyed a 30 year period when they had seldom been without a spinner of note. Of these, only Leslie Townsend, an allrounder of considerable talent before the Second World War, had bowled off spin, but such was the strength of the attack at that time that he often appeared to bowl as an afterthought. Few teams could cope with the pace of Bill Copson, whose health and fitness was the only barrier to a lengthy international career, or the aggression and movement from brothers Alf and George Pope.

Copson was long-limbed and walked with a shuffling gait, but when his body allowed him to do so he could be as quick as anyone in the country for a few overs. Alf Pope was the workhorse, happy to bowl long spells and frequently being asked to, especially in the county's Championship summer of 1936, when his brother was *hors de combat* for most of the season.

George was the craftsman, who had learned to bowl the leg-cutter from the great Sydney Barnes and at times seemed to have the ball on a piece of elastic, one that he pulled this way and that to leave even the best batsmen groping and helpless.

With wickets often suiting their talents, this trio cut a swathe through county batting line-ups throughout the 1930s, but Townsend came into his own when there was any spin – which was often, for away games, as opponents tried to negate the Derbyshire seamers.

He took 1088 first-class wickets between 1922 and 1939 and added, for good measure, 19,555 first-class runs. Yet in that strong bowling line-up, he wasn't regarded as the lead spin bowler.

That title went to Tommy Mitchell. A leg spin bowler with a well-disguised and deadly googly, he took 1483 wickets between 1928 and 1939 at an average of just 20. Bowling with a lively, twirling action, his long fingers enabled him, in the words of former Derbyshire groundsman Walter Goodyear, to 'spin the ball on 'owt'.

He was a mercurial character and sometimes was less than keen to bowl, but his ability to find spin, when there appeared little for anyone else, was appreciated by his captains and team-mates alike.

Although asked to return to the county after the war, Mitchell, by then 43, declined, claiming he could do better working at the colliery and playing as a league professional. This left an opening for the wonderfully named Albert Ennion Groucutt Rhodes, better known to cricket fans as 'Dusty' - or simply 'Bert'.

Rhodes, the father of later Derbyshire seam bowler Harold, was a fine leg spin bowler who had switched from seam bowling with great success.

He had played a few times before the war and was nearly 30 when the county game began again in 1946. For the next seven seasons, until 1952, he proved himself a bowler capable of golden spells that could quickly change matches.

Though taking his wickets more expensively than Tommy Mitchell, Rhodes gave an option when the revered seam attack of Cliff Gladwin and Les Jackson didn't have success. On five occasions he took a hat-trick, although, in common with many of his kind, he could lose line and length on occasion and prove costly in an attack that had otherwise a justified reputation for parsimony.

Rhodes could bat too, but was another whose health and fitness often didn't allow him to fulfil the difficult role of genuine all-rounder to full potential. His best summers with the bat were when his bowling was less of a force and vice versa. By 1951 it was clear that his best days were behind him and that a successor was required.

Which was how, on 6 June 1951, the 17-year old Edwin Smith made his debut for the county, in a game against Hampshire at Queens Park, Chesterfield. It was to become his favourite ground, as it was for many other players on the circuit.

There was much to like in the quaint, small ground in the park. First used by the county in 1898, the Victorian pavilion and rustic scoreboard looked out over a delightful setting. A boating lake at the far end of the ground proved a target for big-hitting batsmen over the years, while musical accompaniment sometimes came from a brass ensemble in the bandstand.

With small boundaries and an outfield that could be fast after a dry spell, Queens Park has usually been a quick-scoring ground, one that could adversely affect the analysis of any bowler without good control of line and length.

Had Edwin seen much cricket at Chesterfield? After all, it wasn't far from his home.

> Actually, I was more of a football fan. I had been to see Chesterfield several times at Saltergate and there were often crowds of around 20,000, that were at that time supervised and monitored by only two policemen!

> I only saw Derbyshire play once before I was in the side. That was in 1946 at Chesterfield against India and I remember seeing Bill Copson open the bowling from the pavilion end. The first ball was so fast I never saw it, then the next was driven back to the pavilion for four by the batsman.

> I was never a cricket watcher. I always enjoyed playing far more than watching and I spent a lot of time that day just walking around the ground. After that I had a job selling ice cream outside Queens Park and I was doing that on the day that George Pope nearly beat Yorkshire on his own in one day.

That was in 1948. Pope took six for 12 in 14 overs, as Yorkshire were dismissed for just 44 before lunch on the first day; then top-scored with 73 as his side took a first innings lead of 233. Incredibly, there was still time for Pope to take two more wickets as Yorkshire subsided to 15 for three by the close, before rain washed out most of the remainder of the game and Yorkshire escaped with an ill-deserved draw.

So how did Edwin feel on his first day in first-class cricket?

> I was nervous. There was no doubting the thrill of being in the same dressing room as people I had read about and trained with, but to change alongside them was something I hadn't really thought about at that point. Perhaps I was included as the local lad, to put a few on the attendance, but to walk out as one of the team ... it was a wonderful feeling that has never left me.

He had to wait to do that, however, as Derbyshire batted well on the first day, one that ended with them on 334 for eight. Rhodes top-scored with 55 and Edwin took his pads off at the end of the day without stepping on to the pitch at number eleven. George Dawkes and Les Jackson shared an unbroken ninth wicket stand of 28, which they extended the next morning before Edwin got in for a brief opportunity. It ended with him unbeaten on nought when the last wicket fell with the total on 356.

When Hampshire batted, there were the near-traditional two early wickets for Les Jackson, but Neville Rogers anchored the innings with an excellent 151 and Hampshire passed 200 with only three wickets down. Rhodes made little impact with his leg spin and Edwin came on to bowl as second-change.

> I knew I could bowl, but the nerves were there. Everyone was really helpful, though. Les told me to take my time and Cliff urged me to make sure that I had my field set just as I wanted it. Guy Willatt was skipper and he was patient and supportive, just what I needed really.

Gladwin worked through the Hampshire innings in a marathon spell that saw him eventually bowl 57 overs and take six for 108, but it wasn't until eight wickets were down that Edwin got his first wicket in first-class cricket.

> I had to wait until the third day. Hampshire batted well down the order and Vic Cannings had helped their wicket-keeper, Leo Harrison, to add 64 for the ninth wicket. Vic eventually went for a big hit off my bowling and the ball sailed down to deep square-leg, where John Kelly held him comfortably. They were 428 for nine at that point, but I had a wicket and that was all that mattered!

The game ended in a draw, the wicket simply too good for a result to be forced. Edwin finished with 19-3-67-1. Nothing to get excited about, perhaps, but he had let no one down.

Another personal triumph for Grassmoor (seven for 18 against Dronfield Prestwick) followed, and a succession of second team engagements, starting with one at Derby against Lincolnshire in the Minor Counties. It is still extraordinary to think that he made his senior bow before playing for the second team, but such fixtures were less common at that time, on grounds of cost. He had only five overs in the first innings, but took two for 44 in the second as the game ended in a draw after its allotted two days. In bowling 22 overs, he showed early signs of the economy and ability to bowl long spells that became a feature of his game.

There was a more chastening experience in his next game for the second team, as a strong Worcestershire side, featuring several players who would become senior regulars in the years ahead, racked up 320 on the first day. Edwin again took two wickets, but they cost him 100 runs as some hefty blows were struck in his 26 overs.

Better news came a few days later at the Crown Farm Colliery Ground at Forest Town, as Derbyshire visited Nottinghamshire for a second team fixture and he took five for 72 in 23 overs.

At the start of August, there was a first visit to Edgbaston for a second team fixture against Warwickshire. The game was severely disrupted by rain, but Edwin's 17 overs saw him take two for 41 and reinforce the feeling that he had something to offer at a senior level. So much so that he was recalled to the first eleven for another fixture at Chesterfield, this time against Worcestershire.

It was a game that Edwin would never forget.

Grassmoor CC 1951 – Back row: Charlie Gladsby, George Hargreaves, Bill Bedford, Jimmy Worthington, Les Towndrow, Tommy Morton, Arthur Bedford Smith (umpire). Front: Wilf Hawkins, Edwin Smith, Ned Bedford, Graham Swift, Jack Seagrave.

In the Derbyshire nets, 1951

Chapter Three

Carnage at Chesterfield

Edwin stepped out of the pavilion for his second match in Derbyshire colours in a more confident mood after those recent performances. He had bowled steadily in his first game and hadn't looked out of his depth, despite the boyish good looks, that he retained throughout his career, making him look like the son of some of the players. Truth be told, he was young enough to be so, but he had been quickly accepted into a Derbyshire dressing room that was open and fun.

Facing them in this match were Worcestershire and they had a number of fine players. Don Kenyon was one of the country's finest opening batsmen, while his partner Eddie Cooper had been a county stalwart since before the war. Sri Lankan 'Laddie' Outschoorn was a good county number three and the side also contained left-arm spinner Dick Howorth, leg spinner Roly Jenkins and seamers Reg Perks and Jack Flavell, who between them took thousands of wickets for the county.

On the first day, Derbyshire did well to restrict their visitors to 268 all out, with the tireless Gladwin taking six for 108 in almost 42 overs, the final wicket being his hundredth of the summer. Les Jackson was injured, but Alwyn Eato bowled steadily in his place and Edwin took the wicket of the experienced Cooper in conceding 54 runs in 15 overs.

Charlie Elliott and Arnold Hamer got through to the close intact and gave their side a steady start the next morning, putting on 39 before Hamer was dismissed to the crowd's disappointment. Always an entertainer but never an athlete, he preferred to deal in boundaries and his cheeks reddened as an innings progressed. He was, however, undoubtedly the linchpin of the side's batting for many seasons. The more conservative Elliott and captain Guy Willatt then took the score to 79 before the spinners started a collapse. An unbeaten 23 from Gladwin helped Derbyshire limp to 141 all out, the innings ending when Edwin was run out as the former tried in vain to keep the strike.

It was the first but not last time that their partnership ended this way. As later skipper Charlie Lee recalled, 'their partnerships usually ended with "Yes!"...."No!"..."Get Back!"..."Oh, bad luck, Edwin."'

A lead of 127 was substantial on a wicket already helping the spinners, but the visitors eased past 50 with only one wicket down. Rhodes, the senior spinner, was surprisingly ineffective with his leg spin so, with the score on 53, Guy Willatt tossed the ball to his young off spinner.

He takes up the story:

It was a right turner! For some reason Bert Rhodes didn't do well on it, so they gave me a go and it started to grip and turn straight away for me. I bowled Don Kenyon when they were 53 for one and then batsmen kept coming in and going out quickly - it was hard to take it all in. They were all out for 78 ...

I remember Cliff Gladwin coming up to me, perhaps after I had my fifth or sixth wicket and saying 'Cometh the hour, Edwin, cometh the man'. He'd used that before, when playing for England during a tight finish in South Africa, but I was overjoyed that all this was happening to me at 17, in my second game in first-class cricket.

I finished with eight for 21 in ten overs ...

Apart from the top three, the highest score for Worcestershire was eight. Kenyon was bowled, but the rest fell in what was to become a regular mode of dismissal – caught in the predatory leg trap, or taken at slip as the ball drifted away. Edwin had bowled out a very good batting side.

It is easy to under-estimate the achievement. For all that conditions were in his favour, the knowledge of that can overawe some bowlers, causing them to get excited and try to do too much with the ball. The old Yorkshire spin bowler, Wilfred Rhodes, once said that 'if batter thinks it's spinnin', it's spinnin''. It was a fair point, as was his assertion that a bowler had only to turn a ball to miss the middle of the bat to have a batsman in trouble.

As he led his team off that evening, Edwin reflected on a job well done, though they knew that the chances of a win were remote: 206 to win on the final day was unlikely and Derbyshire didn't get close. They were all out for 66 in under 30 overs; Perks and Howorth took five wickets each.

A chastened side made the short journey to Nottingham and their next match at Trent Bridge that evening and, as so often, did the unexpected.

They dropped Edwin.

It seems a strange decision even at this distance. What was said to the player to explain it?

Nothing really. Derek Morgan had missed the match at Chesterfield through injury, but it was the sort of thing that was done at that time to stop you getting carried away and full of yourself. Rain ruined the game at Nottingham anyway and seam bowlers took most of the wickets that fell. I went off to play for the second eleven against Lincolnshire and got none for a hundred – so maybe they knew more than I gave them credit for at the time!

He got home to Grassmoor on the bus that evening to find a reporter at the end of the street, wanting his thoughts on the day's play. It was his first encounter with the press and more than anything illustrates the change in both the game and the media. Yet he played only one more game that summer, bowling just six overs in a rain-ruined draw at Derby against Surrey, a side that was to dominate the county cricket scene for most of the decade. At least he had the consolation of returning to his village to

The ball with which Edwin took eight for 21 versus Worcestershire (author).

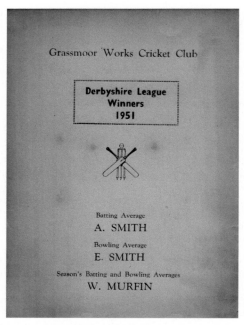

Grassmoor awards night programme, 1951 (Grassmoor CC)

pick up the bowling prize in the club's awards night. It was a fine evening for the Smith family, with his brother, Arthur, picking up the batting prize.

He was selected as twelfth man at Northampton that summer, but didn't make it on to the field. The team stayed in The Angel Hotel and up the road was a snooker hall. The club coach, Denis Smith, went down there one evening and watched a player of undue self-confidence beating a local with ease. At the end of the game, Denis introduced himself and told him that there was a good player in his team, who were staying locally. The player agreed to play him, but when Denis returned a few minutes later, accompanied by Edwin, the man had gone!

Ahead of Edwin lay a winter of work at the colliery. He had enjoyed his taste of county cricket and had showed that he could get good batsmen out. There was much to be done, but he was ready to do whatever was required to become an established county cricketer.

He was surprised at the offers that came his way so early in his career. Derbyshire gave him a £2 a week retainer to ensure he didn't go anywhere else, but he was offered a generous professional contract by Littleborough in the Lancashire League and there were other 'name your price' deals from league clubs, including Kilmarnock in Scotland and several others in the north of England.

He also knew that he faced a challenge from Reg Carter, a slow left-arm bowler of considerable talent. He had played a few games for the second eleven with Edwin in 1951 and at that stage of their development there was little between them in the eyes of some people. The two were good friends, as Edwin explains:

> Reg was a few months older than me and he was a good bowler. The idea was that perhaps the two of us could both play as contrasting spinners. For that to have happened, I think that one of us would have needed to 'kick on' as a batsman, allowing the other to play as a specialist spinner. Reg suffered because they tried to switch him between seam and spin, but he didn't get enough good level cricket to hone his skills.

> We got on really well, though and helped each other as much as we could in the nets.

The highlight of his winter was when Edwin started 'courting', to use the local vernacular. He had known Jean Burton from school, but on a trip to North Wingfield with his brother, ran into her for the first time in a while. That she was pushing a pram was initially a cause for concern, but the baby was that of a friend and Edwin quickly offered to meet her at the cinema in Grassmoor that night.

The response was somewhat non-committal, as she was seeing someone else at the time, but Edwin saved her a seat and she turned up. Can he remember the film? 'No, it wasn't that important,' laughs Edwin, 'but it would have been a cowboy!'

The 1952 season was to be the last for 'Dusty' Rhodes, who bowed out with 83 wickets at just under 25. He played all but two of the 28 matches, although his batting declined from his best years and there were only two half-centuries and an average of 16 from 42 innings. He played a couple of games in 1953 and one in 1954, but his future was planned as an umpire; he stood in eight Test matches between 1963 and 1973. Was he helpful to the young Edwin Smith?

'I didn't see much of him,' said Edwin. 'We were usually in different teams and apart from a few occasions, we were rarely in the same place.'

So who did help him?

> There were a lot of people. Denis Smith was senior professional when I started and he was perfect for the role. He then became coach and was very shrewd and to the point with his advice. Then there was Charlie Elliott and of course Cliff Gladwin. Cliff was a very tetchy player on the field and played to win, but he was a lovely man off it who couldn't do enough to help you. All you had to do was be prepared to listen and learn.

Edwin was in the side for the season opener, against Essex at Chelmsford, but bowled only five overs in a game that, unsurprisingly for an early season wicket, was dominated by the seam bowlers. He took his first wicket of the season in the game against Worcestershire at Chesterfield, but unlike the previous year, Derbyshire eased to a win by nine wickets, thanks to Guy Willatt's century and nine wickets from Cliff Gladwin.

He then missed the next three matches, returning for the annual visit of Yorkshire to Chesterfield. Another Willatt century saw the visitors set 342 to win, but the seam bowlers took two wickets each and Rhodes the other four as Derbyshire ran out winners by 81 runs, despite a battling 91 from Willie Watson. Edwin bowled only eight overs in the match and, as a confirmed number eleven at that time, was hardly in the side for his batting.

It was to be the story of the season. He would play a game, then be omitted for an extra seamer on other wickets, as the captain understandably opted for Rhodes, the senior spinner. When he got an opportunity he did quite well. There were figures of three for 68 in 28 overs against Somerset at Derby, then a recall for an eight wicket win against Northamptonshire at Queens Park, in which he bowled 15 tidy overs for one wicket.

He did feature against the Indian touring side on the same ground, but a rain-ruined first day ensured that a side that showed little technique against pace bowling in the Test series got away with a draw. Les Jackson bowled them out in the first innings for just 86, taking six for 39 in just under 12 overs. Three overs in the second innings hardly justified the selection of the Derbyshire off spinner, in what was proving a frustrating campaign.

There were longer spells in adversity at Taunton, where the punishing Somerset opening batsman, Harold Gimblett, scored two centuries. The game ended in a high-scoring draw, with Edwin taking two wickets in each innings. It was a warm-up for his next match at Wellingborough School against Northamptonshire, where the spinners came into their own as the season moved into late summer.

Edwin took five for 49 as Northamptonshire made 219 on the first day, then four for 51 in the second innings, as his side were left 194 to win, which they achieved for the loss of five wickets. It was the first time since his magical spell at Chesterfield the previous summer that he had out-bowled Rhodes.

He played in four more games that season, though in each had little chance to shine. There were two wickets in each innings against Surrey at The Oval, but his side was heavily beaten by a strong side and Edwin was dismissed for his first 'pair' in the first-class game, bowled by Tony Lock in the first innings and Alec Bedser in the second.

He had, at least, moved up the batting order by the end of the season, swapping places with Les Jackson and going in at number ten. It was the start of an improvement in his batting that would gradually see him become a doughty fighter in the lower middle order for the county.

A typical Smith-Gladwin run out.
Edwin is on the floor as Gladwin looks mystified.
Don Shepherd is the Glamorgan bowler, Haydn Davies the wicket-keeper.

Chapter Four

First team regular – and capped

Nineteen-fifty three was a momentous year. England won back the Ashes and Edwin Smith became a first team regular for Derbyshire for the first time.

Edwin played 18 games for Derbyshire in that Coronation summer, that ended with the county sixth in the table. Four batsmen passed the thousand-run barrier, led by Arnold Hamer, who came close to 1500 in his trademark style. Meanwhile, Cliff Gladwin bowled over a thousand overs in the Championship, taking 121 wickets at 18 runs each and conceding just two runs an over in the process. Les Jackson just missed his hundred wickets, while Derek Morgan took 64 with a mixture of medium pace and off cutters.

It was a fine side. The batting could be sketchy at times, but when Hamer got going the crowd enjoyed the spectacle. Thirty-three before he played regular county cricket, he scored a thousand runs in ten successive seasons and always played with one eye on the scoreboard and the other on the crowd and their entertainment. Not until the advent of Kim Barnett many years later did the county have an English batsman of similar approach and there was a discernible disappointment among supporters when he was dismissed early.

John Kelly came from the other side of the Pennines to Hamer, but the Lancastrian gave sterling service, mainly as a more dour opener who served as the perfect counterfoil. Alan Revill was another who sometimes fired off strokes with disregard for his average, but played many important innings and, for a naturally aggressive batsman, was remarkably consistent for several seasons.

The Repton-educated Donald Carr would eventually take over the captaincy from Guy Willatt. Both were fine players with a good range of strokes and in turn would lead the side with unruffled temperament and no little skill.

Providing ballast to the batting was Derek Morgan, one of the finest all-rounders never to represent his country. While not a graceful player, Morgan was functional and a fighter, usually contributing runs when they were most needed or when scoring them was at its most difficult. His bowling gradually became an important component of a fine attack, he and Edwin becoming team mates for the best part of 20 seasons.

They were a tight band and, for all that there were strong characters among them, they got on well. At 19, Edwin was lead spinner in the county side and understandably found things difficult at times. As Guy Willatt wrote in the 1954 club yearbook:

> Smith was as accurate and, when the wicket helped him, as effective as ever, but due to the departure of Rhodes he was necessarily called upon to bowl on wickets unsuited to his style and, lacking sufficient variety or experience, had little success.

He continued with mention of a threat to his place:

> Carter latterly showed he had real promise and if he can bowl with increasing accuracy, might prove the left-hander sought after for many years.

Perhaps the captain was being unfairly critical of Carter. He had bowled 88 overs in the summer and had taken 12 wickets at an average of just 16 runs each, conceding less than three runs an over. It showed the high expectations of young bowlers in a disciplined attack.

Carter got into the side in August and, at the age of 19, took two wickets in each innings as Derbyshire beat Leicestershire at Derby by ten wickets. Better was to follow at Chesterfield, on a wicket that Edwin would undoubtedly have enjoyed, as the home side beat Somerset by an innings and 82 runs. Carter took seven successive wickets in the second innings, ending with figures of 19-7-46-7. It was to prove the highpoint of his brief career, but at the end of the summer Edwin was well aware that he had a fight on his hands for the role of first-choice spinner

> Reg and I were good friends. We bowled a similar style, albeit with different hands and worked together in the nets, encouraging each other on and trying out different things. Where I ended up winning was that I was more accurate and could generally be relied upon to keep it tight when we were waiting on a new ball, or just wanting to give Cliff and Les a breather.

> My batting also came on more quickly and so I had more to offer. Reg had hard luck though and at another time could have been given greater opportunity.

Edwin's best performance of the summer had come against the visiting Australians at Chesterfield. On a soft wicket, where play didn't start until after lunch on the first day, the visitors were dismissed for 197, Gladwin taking five wickets and Jackson three. Only Richie Benaud's aggressive 70 saved them from embarrassment. It was Derbyshire's turn to struggle on the second day, being dismissed for just 69.

Second time around, Australia did better and at 88 for two looked set for a big score, but as soon as Edwin came on to partner Cliff Gladwin, the wickets started to fall. Both opener Colin McDonald and Benaud were bowled by what were described as 'magnificent balls' and the innings became a procession. Australia were all out for 146 and thus made their two lowest scores of the tour at that point. Edwin's analysis was 16-3-36-5 and he claimed some notable scalps among his victims, all of them despite a badly bruised spinning finger, sustained when attempting a diving catch

Derbyshire versus Australia, Chesterfield, 1953.

Derbyshire squad versus Worcestershire at Worcester 1954.
Back: David Green, Arnold Hamer, Les Jackson. Arthur Robson (physio),
Derek Morgan, Reg Carter, John Kelly, Edwin Smith.
Front: George Dawkes, Donald Carr, Guy Willatt, Cliff Gladwin, Alan Revill.

on the boundary.

The press were effusive in their praise. 'Edwin Smith is a remarkable young bowler,' wrote former Australian opening batsman Jack Fingleton, while his erstwhile team mate, the legendary Bill O'Reilly, was even more enthusiastic. He deemed it 'a stirring display of highly-intelligent bowling' - praise indeed, from a man regarded as one of the game's greats.

Rain prevented Derbyshire making an attempt on a winning target of 275 on the final day, the game ending in a draw. Yet Edwin had perhaps his most encouraging figures yet and more reason to feel he could make the grade as a county cricketer.

What he needed was a solid season to cement his place. He had taken 28 wickets at 35; steady but not spectacular and Reg Carter had taken half that number of wickets in 400 fewer overs, albeit with the benefit of bowling on the most spin-friendly wicket of the summer. In finishing sixth with such an inexperienced seam attack, the county had exceeded expectations.

It was perhaps unrealistic of Derbyshire to place the role of lead spin bowler in the hands of a young man still in his teens; his back up, Carter, only two months older. Yet the reality was that for much of that decade, Cliff Gladwin and Les Jackson reigned supreme. There were few occasions when both failed to take wickets. Usually one or the other could find sufficient movement to get among the opposition batsmen and when wickets were falling they were happy to keep bowling.

The groundsman at Derby during this period was the legendary Walter Goodyear. He had taken over the role in 1938 and, returning to his duties after the war, he remained in charge of wickets at the County Ground until his retirement in 1982. What were they like? Walter explains.

> They got a Walter Goodyear wicket and for a long time I prepared them specifically for Les Jackson. People used to turn up for matches and ask me how it would play. My answer was usually the same. 'If we win the toss we'll put the buggers in and Les will have three or four wickets before lunch'.
>
> He usually did, you know. If he didn't, I was for it!

It was much the same at Chesterfield, where the majority of home matches were played at that time. While the ball turned more than at Derby, where only in the last couple of sessions of a game could a spinner expect to come into his own, generations of seam bowlers smiled in anticipation of a trip to Queen's Park.

Edwin returned to Grassmoor for the winter of 1953, and returned to the County Ground in April 1954 knowing that he had a big season ahead of him. Escape from year-round work at the pit was possible, but first he needed to cement a place in the Derbyshire side.

Pre-season training began a few weeks before the cricket itself. Most of the players kept fit by a range of manual jobs and got fit for playing cricket by doing just that. Nor was there the extensive pre-match warm-up that modern supporters take for granted. It was written of the Hampshire legend, Derek Shackleton that his warm-up consisted of 'combing his hair and having a fag'. Derbyshire's players might take a few catches from the slip cradle or from the bat of the coach, but their greater energies were reserved for the field of play.

The season began on 8 May, two days after Roger Bannister became the first man to break the four-minute mile, at Oxford. Derbyshire set off at a fair pace themselves, beating Leicestershire at Derby after bowling out their visitors on the first day for 134. Edwin took four for 17 in seven overs, before the Gladwin-Jackson combination ensured there was no way back, sharing all ten wickets in the second innings, as Derbyshire won easily by seven wickets.

It was an encouraging start and was to prove an excellent season for the county. They finished in third place, but in an exceptionally wet summer they had the worst of the weather, especially as the season drew to a climax. With four games left, they were favourites for the title, just six points behind Yorkshire who had only two games remaining. Yet the rain ruined the county's next two games, when they were in good positions.

It was the pinnacle of Guy Willatt's captaincy and he resigned his post at the end of the summer to become headmaster of Heversham Grammar School. He had moulded a fine team, in the process abolishing the segregation of the amateur and professional at the club, where amateurs previously stayed in different hotels, changed separately and sat at different tables to eat. Edwin rated him very highly.

> Guy Willatt was the best captain I played under, without question. He was a messy bloke in the dressing room and used to shake his gear out of his cricket bag onto the floor, where it would be crumpled, stained and creased! But he was a terrific captain and set some innovative and imaginative fields for everyone. He was a very good batsman too and was missed when he retired.
>
> As players we had total confidence in him and that was a big thing. Cliff wanted to win, at everything he did and was never slow to speak out, but he respected Guy Willatt and that said a lot about him.
>
> Donald Carr, who took over, was a good skipper too, but we felt that he thought if Les and Cliff couldn't bowl teams out, it wasn't going to happen. He could be slow to bowl himself too and that cost us on occasions. I think he was a better bowler than he gave himself credit for.

Gladwin and Jackson both took well over a hundred wickets in the summer, but it was the emergence of Edwin Smith as a genuine county spinner that caught the eye. He took 71 wickets at 20 runs each, conceding just over two runs an over in the process. His captain was impressed:

> Smith bowled as accurately as ever, but introduced an element of variety into his attack, hitherto lacking. On hard, fast wickets where

he could not turn the ball he took wickets by subtle variations of flight and direction, worthy of a much older head.

Edwin, like Derek Morgan, also received praise for 'bowling to orders' and their ability to keep things tight while the opening attack rested proved a key component of a successful season. He again did well against the touring side, on this occasion Pakistan, taking two wickets in their first innings, then making his top score so far of an unbeaten 40, as he and Reg Carter added a crucial last wicket stand of 65 to avoid the follow-on.

The season was made all the more memorable by a first win against Yorkshire at Headingley since 1895, Hamer's batting and Morgan's bowling the deciding factors in a display that was 'celebrated in more ways than one' according to Edwin. The win was indicative of the professionalism of the side, as he explains.

> Arnold looked on a different level to everyone else when we made 272. He carried his bat for 147 not out and really enjoyed that, against the county of his birth. Cliff hit Len Hutton on the hand in their innings and with the ball lifting and moving around, they were all out for 119.

> They did a little better in the second innings, when they followed on, but we knew Len had gone to hospital for an x-ray. Cliff kept saying to us 'Come on, he's going to come back and bat lower down, we need to get them out before he can do that'. As it turned out, Len had broken a finger and couldn't bat, but Cliff missed very little on a cricket field and wasn't going to miss out on an opportunity like that.

Edwin's personal highlight was the award of his county cap, at the end of the second game against Yorkshire at Chesterfield on 15 June. He took five for 37 in 20 overs as Yorkshire collapsed in the first innings, but the game ended in a draw with the game well balanced. What difference did the cap make?

> It was a recognition of achievement and in my case, of a series of good displays. There was no fuss, as that wasn't the way things were done. I was simply presented with it in the dressing room at the end of the game. Having said that, I was only on £400 for the season and financially I was better off earning the £8 per match fee for occasional call-ups and working at Grassmoor.

> The basic salary meant that you had to be creative with your expenses claims. If we were playing locally, at Leicester or Nottingham, some would claim hotel expenses but go back home. One time we played a match at Ilkeston and Cliff Gladwin gave Les, myself and Jim Brailsford a lift to the game in his car.

> Will Taylor asked us for our expenses after the game and Les and I both claimed bus fares, which we gave to Cliff for the petrol. Jim said 'It's all right Mr Taylor, I got a lift with Cliff'.

> Well, you should have seen Cliff's face. When Mr Taylor had gone, he turned to Jim and said 'Do you think my bloody car runs on water?'

The confidence that Edwin got from such a successful season and the award of his cap sent him into the winter content. In some quarters he was being spoken of as a potential England player, the former Gloucestershire off-spinner Tom Goddard pronouncing him 'the best young spin bowler I have seen this summer'.

It gave him something to build on in 1955.

Legendary club groundsman Walter Goodyear and Donald Carr at the County Ground.

Chapter Five

A hundred wickets

Edwin wasn't the only one with building plans in 1955. The County Ground got an overhaul over the winter and the club's new indoor cricket school opened on 17 January, the ceremony being performed by the MCC assistant secretary S.C.Griffith. While not unduly spacious, with little room for bowler run ups, it was appreciated by the players.

The season began with a home fixture against the touring South African side and saw the revamped County Ground declared officially open by the Duke of Devonshire. The game was played on the new square, which was now on the side of the ground that adjoined the Grandstand Hotel, bringing spectators much closer to the action. A new press box, changing facilities in the converted old jockey quarters on the racecourse and the demolition of the old pavilion gave the ground a new look. In front of the grandstand, new terracing to accommodate 3,500 members had been prepared.

It augured well for the season, but the county slipped to eighth, suffering ten defeats. The number three slot vacated by Guy Willatt proved a problem all summer. Yorkshireman Charlie Lee had been specially registered for that position, but had suffered a broken leg playing football and was never fully fit. Various options were tried, none of them proving satisfactory. While Arnold Hamer and new skipper Donald Carr enjoyed prolific summers, Willatt finished top of the averages on his return to the side in the school holidays, reinforcing what was missed.

Even worse was the shoulder injury that kept Les Jackson out of half of the season. He still finished top of the county averages, with 64 wickets at 14, but his absence placed an additional burden on the other bowlers. Cliff Gladwin rose to the challenge, taking 142 wickets at less than 15 and conceding under two runs an over, while Edwin enjoyed what was to be his most prolific summer.

Much was down to increased opportunity, as he bowled 200 overs more than in the previous year, but his strike-rate and economy were also improved and Edwin became established as a key member of the Derbyshire attack. Hour after hour of sunshine in a golden summer dried out wickets and helped him too, but the confidence of being a capped player at 21 helped to make him, in the words of Donald Carr 'one of the best off spin bowlers in the country'.

Support came from Carr, whose left-arm unorthodox spin took 43 wickets. The nature of his bowling meant that there could be occasional, sometimes frequent, loose balls, yet these seemed to acquire an additional potency in

Telegram received from Les Jackson on reaching 100 wickets.

Pre-season training 1955: Sam Weaver, Edwin and Alan Revill lead the way, closely followed by Morgan and Dawkes. Hamer working hard to the rear.

the light of the parsimony from elsewhere.

While Derek Morgan had a summer where his bowling struggled for rhythm, time and again Gladwin and Edwin bowled long, accurate and penetrative spells to keep their team in games. A glance at the scorecards of the summer shows how remarkably accurate this young bowler was, evidenced not just by his economy but by the number of victims bowled and leg-before.

> I used to bowl very close to the stumps and aim for a spot just outside off at the other end. By getting in so close, I only had to turn the ball a little to beat the middle of the bat and if the batsman left a 'gate' I had a good chance of getting through and bowling him.

Worcestershire were again victims, this time at Worcester. Six for 45 in 22 overs, five of them bowled and one caught at slip, before Gladwin and Carr made short work of their second innings for an easy win. At Bristol, Gloucestershire narrowly avoided defeat, despite Edwin's figures of 18-9-29-3 and 18-3-39-5. Back at Chesterfield, he took six for 69 in 38 overs against Essex (four bowled) and three for 14 in eight overs in the second innings.

Four for 34 in 16 overs against Glamorgan was followed by a less prolific but equally meritorious effort against Lancashire, when a 40-over spell conceded just 52 runs for two wickets, while the Jackson-Gladwin combination took the rest of the wickets at the other end. At Leicester, on a good batting wicket where the game ended in a high scoring draw, he took three for 17 in 18 overs. These were the figures of an experienced bowler, not a relative rookie.

His greatest memory of that summer came in the following game, against Nottinghamshire at Trent Bridge. Derbyshire had only previously won twice on this ground and with the prolific Australian leg spin bowler Bruce Dooland in their ranks, the home side would have fancied their chances. Edwin takes up the story.

> Arnold Hamer was a wonderful batsman. He could be susceptible to the swinging ball early in his innings, like most players are, but when he got going he was a fine sight, as long as you weren't bowling to him!

> He had a great record against Nottinghamshire and their opening bowler, Arthur Jepson, would usually offer him 50 runs if he stayed in the dressing room. That day, Arnold raced to fifty, but from 94 for one we slid to 133 for seven when I went in. Bruce Dooland had just taken three wickets in seven balls and the ball was spinning a long way for the first day of the game.

> I went in at number nine and Arnold just told me to stay there, while he did the rest. I did that for a while, but then started playing some shots of my own. Almost before I knew it, I had 50 on the board and that was my first for Derbyshire.

> I had the best view in the house of Arnold in full flow and he treated

the attack almost with disdain.

The pair added 157 runs in 89 minutes, completely changing the game. Derbyshire ended with 354, of which Hamer hit 227 (five sixes and 27 fours) and Edwin a precious 57 with eight boundaries. He and Gladwin bowled out Nottinghamshire the following day and after heavy rain that evening, Derbyshire won by 111 runs on the last day.

Then it was back to Chesterfield, where his second innings five for 22 was not enough to prevent a Hampshire win. There followed two games in which he had only two wickets, before Derbyshire headed to Edinburgh on the overnight sleeper, for a three-day game against Scotland.

Gladwin was rested and Jackson injured, so Brian Furniss, from Baslow, made his debut and took the new ball with Derek Hall. Scotland batted solidly and amassed 289, with Edwin taking five for 66 in 39 overs. Then Guy Willatt's fine century showed what the county were missing, as Derbyshire took a first innings lead of one run. Edwin takes over the story.

> Scotland moved nicely to 45 without loss before I took the first wicket and then it became a procession. Most of them went to the leg trap as I took the first nine wickets to fall on a turning wicket.

> Then, with the last pair together, the batsman hit one back at me. It wasn't easy, but I should have held it. Arnold Hamer, who was bowling his off spin at the other end, came up to me and said 'Well, if you don't want it, I'll have it' and took the last wicket in the next over!

Nine for 46 in 26 overs gave Edwin match figures of 14 for 112 and Derbyshire eased to a win by eight wickets, aided by John Kelly being dropped four times.

The steady bowling continued to the end of the season and six for 80 against Sussex, albeit in a losing cause, reinforced Edwin's case for international consideration. He had passed the hundred wicket mark for the first time and proved himself a bowler capable of getting teams out when conditions suited, as well as keeping them quiet when the batsmen held sway. His name was mentioned in press circles as a likely tourist for Pakistan in 1955-56, a side that would be captained by his county skipper, Donald Carr.

Serious consideration was still a thing for the future, but a congratulatory telegram from Les Jackson, on achieving his hundred wicket milestone, took pride of place in his souvenirs from the season.

Chapter Six
Being a professional

The lot of the professional cricketer in the 1950s was substantially different to that of their modern day counterparts. Go to any first-class cricket ground today and you will see an array of impressive cars, some of them sponsored, a number with personalised plates and all of them a reflection of the trappings of success. County cricketers may not be as well paid as footballers, but many would envy the lifestyle.

It was not always so. Take getting to the ground, simply for a home game, as Edwin explains.

> I used to have to get a bus from Grassmoor to Chesterfield at 7.40am and then get the so-called 'pigeon train' to Derby. It stopped at Clay Cross, Belper, Ambergate and Duffield and it was really slow. It got me to Derby around 9.40am and then I had to get a bus outside the station into Derby town centre and then another that took me to Nottingham Road and the cricket ground.

> If it all went to plan I would get there around 10.15am. Of course, at the end of the day, you had to do it all again, in reverse. Les Jackson got a car in 1956 and then Cliff Gladwin got one and they used to give me lifts, which saved a lot of time.

> I had a Lambretta scooter for a while, but it wasn't easy, and probably not very safe, travelling on that with my cricket gear!

When Edwin joined the Derbyshire staff, no equipment was provided. Once capped, the club provided his blazer and sweaters in club colours, but prior to that he wore a cricket sweater knitted by Jean, his girlfriend and eventual wife. He bought his own boots, pads and batting gloves, but got a free bat from Gunn and Moore, as long as he purchased one. All the players were the same. Those lucky enough to play for more affluent counties and gain international recognition perhaps did better, but sponsorship for most players was some way in the future.

Later, the players benefited from one of Cliff Gladwin's many contacts. He arranged for cricket trousers to be made by Jack Berry, a mill-owner friend in Bradford, from a gabardine material, 'far better than the ordinary cricket trousers of the time' according to Edwin. Cliff later called on the same friend for the material for Jean's wedding dress, in 1956.

> We were lucky enough to do what thousands of others would have wanted to do. There were plenty of people back in Grassmoor who would have willingly traded places with me, being able to play cricket

for six months of the year. I think most of the players from that background appreciated that running around in the daylight and fresh air was a much better option.

Edwin, in common with most of the Derbyshire professionals, earned around £400 a season until he was capped. Before he got to that stage, his spell on the ground staff had opened his eyes to the lot of the would-be professional.

We used to have to erect the wooden tiered seating that was transported around the grounds before every game and if there were nets, we used to put them up as well. On a Monday morning Walter Goodyear cut and prepared four nets at Derby, two of them shaved for the spinners and the others with more grass for the seam bowlers. Then we'd brush them and they'd be rolled and cut again before use.

We would do a range of chores around the ground and then practice ourselves. Finally, between 5.30pm and 7.30pm, we had to bowl at the members who turned up for a 20-minute net.

Edwin's shoulders start to shake and a chuckle breaks out, as he remembers some of those sessions from long ago:

Oh, we had some laughs! There was one member, a chap named Potter, who turned up every night on a push bike with his cricket kit. He even turned up one evening with his arm in a cast, having broken it.

Keith Mohan and myself were egging Harold Rhodes on to bowl fast and hit his other one, so we could get the next night off!

They used to get 20 minutes of batting each. Some of them were quite good and I remember some of the Repton public school lads came down. There was also a policeman named Alec Macbeth, who was a big chap and hit the ball very hard.

I used to toss the ball up to him and he'd hit me for miles. I worked out quickly that if I took my time on the way for the ball and back, I'd only have to bowl one or two deliveries at him ...

At the end of it all, of course, was the journey home that I mentioned earlier, so they were long, but happy days.

Progression from the ground staff was the goal, but the young players had to work hard, with tough taskmasters in groundsman Walter Goodyear and coach Denis Smith. Neither suffered fools gladly, but they had jobs to do and worked hard. The two men were good friends, as Walter explains:

Denis and I got on brilliantly. We always did when he was a player, but when he became coach we had a lot of fun. He always had his pipe on the go – you rarely saw him without it – and we never had a cross word. I always knew where he was from the plume of smoke from that pipe!

I remember one time he broke my finger by accident and I had to go to the hospital to get it splinted. The next day I was lifting something and

Edwin.

More pre-season work: Edwin, Alan Revill and Laurie Johnson on the front row, with Derek Hall, Arnold Hamer and Gordon Beet behind.

I dropped it, while trying to protect my injured finger. It landed on his foot and broke his toe! Oh, we had some laughs about that...

As coach, Denis Smith was gruff and abrasive, rarely short of a pithy comment when one was required. A would-be quick bowler, leaving the car park in a hurry with engine roaring after a trial 'wouldn't hit anything, if he drives like he bowls'. Another player, resplendent in a new suit and perhaps a little full of himself, was told 'that old suit of mine has scrubbed up well'.

The coach's attitude came from graduating through a tough school himself. The Derbyshire side of the 1930s was as combative an eleven as ever took the field for the county. 'No one wants molly-coddling, there's no one to hold your hand in the middle,' was a regular response to those who questioned his severity at times. He perhaps recalled occasions such as when George Pope, batting against Yorkshire's testing attack of that pre-war period, swung hard at a delivery and sent it whistling past the head of Brian Sellers, the captain, fielding at forward short leg.

'I say Pope, I think you tried to hit me there,' he said, as the ball sped away.

'You keep fielding there Mr Sellers. You'll be in no doubt next time...' came the reply.

Smith was a shrewd coach, with sound, practical ideas, as remembered by Alan Hill, a fine opening batsman of later vintage for the county.

> Denis was gruff, but his bark was worse than his bite. He could be blunt, but he had played the game and knew all of its pitfalls. If you had a bad day he would empathise with you, as long as he could see that you were putting the effort in.
>
> He taught me things, long before the days of videos and statistical analysis and I still use them when I coach. If you study top professional cricketers, perhaps the most important thing is balance. When I wasn't playing well, I started to fall over to the off side and got out lbw.
>
> He came up to me in the nets during such a trot and said, in his broad Derbyshire accent 'Ey up ... when tha' walks down street, what position is tha' head in?' I was baffled and showed him.
>
> 'Exactly,' he said. 'Now try doin' it with tha' head to one side.'
>
> I couldn't and it showed perfectly and succinctly where I was going wrong.

On and off the pitch, discipline was important and throughout the 1950s was 'enforced' by the senior professional, Cliff Gladwin. Young players were taken under his wing, but were expected to listen and learn, as Edwin explains.

> Cliff came off at the intervals and knew his analysis to the run. It was extraordinary. He would sit down and announce his work for the session 'Twelve overs, five maidens, three for 17' or similar. Then he'd

look at anyone who had dropped a catch and say 'It would have been four for 17 if this so-and-so hadn't missed that one'.

You dreaded dropping one off Cliff. You would never hear the end of it and he would call you all the names under the sun. But we didn't mind, because it showed his commitment and he was a wonderful bowler. He loved his maiden overs and if he had bowled five balls without conceding a run, there was no way a batsman would score off the sixth!

Indeed, Gladwin came into his own in times of adversity, willing and able to bowl long spells with a short, skipping run and an astonishing ability to control a cricket ball, fondly remembered by Edwin.

He was probably just short of international class, to be honest, but at county level, with three short leg fielders, his ability to put the ball on a length was unbelievable, while his stamina enabled him to bowl all day.

He was unlike any other bowler of his kind. Nearly all of them swung it into the batsman from the hand, so you saw it swinging all the way. Cliff's deliveries looked as if they were going straight until halfway down the wicket and then they would swing or jag into the batsman, bringing the short legs into play. He developed a very good leg cutter too and got many caught behind or in the slips as the batsmen played for the expected swing.

Such was Gladwin's versatility, that Edwin sometimes suffered, when conditions would have been in his favour.

There was one wicket at Northampton in the mid-50s and when we got there it looked really green. There was little difference between the wicket and the rest of the square and outfield. When we went out to see it up close, it was just grass clippings on top of sand! It was obviously going to turn square and I fancied my chances of a long bowl.

The thing was, so did Cliff! When he got a little tired, he cut down his pace and bowled off-cutters, so I didn't get to bowl that many! There was another time at Worcester, when the usual winter floods had left a kind of silt on the wicket. Cliff said that he'd bowl at one end to break the wicket up for me – and he bowled them out. If there was any help in the wicket at all, Cliff would bowl whatever was required for as long as necessary. He was a dream for a captain, because you often only had to think about changing one end.

Like Les Jackson, Gladwin was indebted to Alan Revill, Donald Carr and Derek Morgan, who were as good in the leg trap as any in the country. Edwin was also grateful for their ability.

Some of the catches they held weren't really chances, but their reactions were astonishing and they picked up some outrageous ones. I remember Alan holding one from a full-blooded pull once. We were all looking to the boundary and then turned to see him throwing the ball up, cool as you like. I was lucky to have people capable of such brilliance in the team, as all the bowlers were.

Travel around the country at that time was arduous and time-consuming. Jackson and Gladwin, as befitted their status, were among the first in the team to buy cars, but for most, travel was a case of jumping on a bus or a train, especially to away matches. When he was one of the junior players, Edwin was tasked with ensuring that the player's cricket gear got to the ground for away fixtures.

We all used to meet at the station and one of the junior members of the side would have picked up the tickets from Mr Taylor, the secretary. Once there, our job was to load all the cricket bags and anything the players didn't want with them on to trolleys, then get these to the right platform and then on to the train.

Once we were on board we would relax and there would be a few card schools going. When we got to the other end, we had to get everything off the train, back on to trolleys and then sort taxis – some for the players and at least one, sometimes two, for the equipment. You had to keep your wits about you, but I only remember things being messed up once.

We were coming back from a game up north and we got the bags on the guard's van of the train. I told Derek Morgan that I would be jumping off at Chesterfield and would pick them up the next morning at Derby, if he got them off at the other end.

What we didn't know was that they had changed the guard's van to a Birmingham train! We had to go down to the station the next morning, wait for the Birmingham train to arrive and unload the bags into taxis, then go to the ground where we were playing. There wasn't much time to spare.

Arnold had a big van for a while, which he used for his winter job. That made life a lot easier for the young players, but there were times when he wasn't allowed to drive a long distance and the part-time porter work began again!

If they got there in good time, the players would have an evening meal at the hotel. If the transport plans went awry and they arrived too late, they would go to a local Berni Inn for a steak, always a favourite. When they were in London, a group would always head to the cinema at Marble Arch and wherever they went, nothing was done to excess, as Edwin explains.

Going out for a drink was exactly that ... one drink.

Cliff made sure of that and made a point of telling us 'You have ONE', holding up a finger to reinforce the point. No one ever crossed him, they wouldn't have dared, because he was a big man. None of them were big drinkers, to be honest and I only drank a milk stout until I was about 26. I'd nurse a half pint all night, the others might take a pint, but we were always in bed by eleven. Always.

The game itself was different. On the field, players were aware of their roles and there was little to no expectation of bowlers diving around.

Both Les and Cliff were decent fielders, with a good pair of hands and decent arms. Les was especially good off his own bowling. He rarely bowled with a mid off, because he kept it short of a length so they couldn't drive him. On several occasions I saw him run out batsmen at the non-striker's end, when they thought they had hit the ball past him. He would swoop down quickly, stop it with his left hand, transfer quickly to the right and throw down the stumps.

When it happened once we thought it a fluke, but he did it too often for that. As bowlers, we were deemed too important to the side to be diving to stop balls and potentially damage a shoulder or whatever. If it was near us, we did our best, but you seldom saw people diving to stop fours on the boundary. Closer to the wicket was different and I've rarely seen better close fielders than Derek Morgan, Alan Revill and Donald Carr.

Off the field, players mixed at the end of the day's play and chatted about life on the circuit, new players and the ones who had impressed them. It was an unofficial schooling for a young bowler like Edwin.

There were so many good off spinners around. You'd struggle to name three good ones in the county game today, but there were three at Gloucestershire at the same time! They had John Mortimore, David Allen and 'Bomber' Wells, all very fine bowlers. Tom Goddard had only recently retired there too.

Then there was the great Jim Laker at Surrey, as well as the under-rated Eric Bedser. Yorkshire had Ray Illingworth and Brian Close, Middlesex had Fred Titmus and Lancashire had Roy Tattersall. Wherever you played there was a good spinner and it was a magical time to play the game.

At the end of the day we'd sit down with a pint and talk over the play, chat about different players on the circuit and how we bowled to them. You learned a lot from these sessions – as you had to do, picking the brains of people who were so good at their craft.

I used to love the various festivals around the country, when you could go into the beer tent at the end of the day and relax. They were great times.

It was hard work and there was little financial reward, yet a period remembered with fondness for the characters that he played with and the friendships made. Of many funny stories, Edwin still chuckles at one that featured the irrepressible Gladwin.

Alan Revill had been batting on a fiery pitch and had edged a ball into his chin, which was bleeding profusely as he returned to the pavilion. A local doctor was summoned and, quickly realising that stitches were required, he asked for a half bottle of whiskey to be purchased.

He sterilised the wound with it and gave Alan a few swigs prior to starting his work. A few stitches later, he said he was done and turned around for the bottle to give Alan a couple more swigs to numb the pain.

Cliff had drunk the lot! The game was in the bag anyway, but we all laughed, including Alan, until he realised that it hurt too much ...

Chapter Seven

Ashes summer

Mention the year 1956 to most cricket fans and their first thought will be of the Ashes series, an English triumph and Jim Laker. The summer proved one of the wettest on record.

Derbyshire finished sixth from bottom, but lost 121 hours to rain and bad weather and the cold, gloom and wind, aside from the rain, meant that county attendances were considerably down. Indeed, Derbyshire ended the season with a large deficit, losing two Saturdays at Chesterfield, the Saturday of the Nottinghamshire 'derby' at Ilkeston and all but 49 overs against Hampshire at Chesterfield, where the visitors limped to 59 for seven in that time. The Worcestershire game at the same venue saw only eight overs of play in three days.

The season overview by Donald Carr in the following summer's yearbook made for equally gloomy reading. While acknowledging the sterling efforts of Jackson and Gladwin once more, the captain noted that their 'advancing years may tend to reduce their stamina'.

His concern for players coming through in different areas is also clear, while acknowledging the potential of seam bowlers Harold Rhodes, Derek Hall and Brian Furniss. The last two failed to realise that potential, while Rhodes went on to be one of the county's finest players, as well as one shamefully treated by the cricket authorities.

'Les and Cliff' both passed the hundred wicket mark, devastating when the weather allowed play on rain-affected wickets, but hindered by the loss of the best part of 20 days' play over the summer.

For Edwin Smith, the wicket tally reduced to 59 at a shade under 30 runs each, leaving him the third top wicket-taker It was disappointing after the previous summer, but he bowled over 200 overs fewer and the frequent stoppages meant that the two main seam bowlers could bowl frequent spells, with the benefit of a break in the pavilion. His performances were steady and there were few spells when he was 'collared', but opportunities to run through sides rarely presented themselves.

Having excelled in Scotland in 1955, his season's best came in Wales. The game against Glamorgan, at Swansea's St Helen's ground, saw Edwin reduce the home side from 124 for three to 188 all out, taking seven for 58. Another Hamer masterclass of 120 saw Derbyshire take a first innings lead of 69, but only Jim Presdee, with an unbeaten 59, resisted Edwin and Derek Morgan for long. The home side were dismissed for 137, Edwin taking four for 57 in 21 overs of what was called 'accurate and controlled

Derbyshire at Chesterfield 1956. Back: Gerry Wyatt, John Kelly, Charlie Lee, Harold Rhodes, Les Jackson, Derek Morgan, Laurie Johnson, Edwin Smith. Front: Arnold Hamer, Cliff Gladwin, Donald Carr (captain) George Dawkes.

Swindon Cricket Club Dinner 1956: Jackson, Revill, Edwin and Gladwin with the organiser.

spin bowling'.

There were six wickets for 52 runs as he bowled out Somerset on the last afternoon at Derby, but the damp, seam-friendly conditions meant he bowled only a wicketless 20 overs in the match against the Australians at Derby. The visitors won that match by 57 runs, largely thanks to two fine innings by Ian Craig and a fine last afternoon spell by Keith Miller.

Edwin's season was extended with two games for the MCC. The first, at Lord's in May, saw him bowl only eight overs, but in the second, against Yorkshire at the Scarborough Festival, he took three wickets as his side was heavily beaten.

After that game, he had to catch the midnight train to make an appearance for the North against the South at Torquay. Poor weather meant there was only play on the first day and neither Edwin, nor his county team mates Alan Revill and Cliff Gladwin, got onto the pitch.

There was an interesting interlude as the players sat in the pavilion watching the rain, as he explains:

> 'Jock' Livingston was a mainstay of Northamptonshire's side in the 1950s and scored thousands of runs for them, after initially moving from Australia to play in the leagues. He and George Tribe were the stars of a decent side, one that had been put together by recruits from other counties and from those who undertook a qualification period to play county cricket from overseas.

> He asked me for a word and said that Northamptonshire were interested in securing my services. Would I consider it? Their wickets usually favoured spin bowling and perhaps such conditions might have earned me more bowling and more wickets; maybe greater recognition from selectors. But I firmly believed then, and still do, that players should only be eligible for their county of birth.

> So I told Jock thanks, but I wasn't interested – and that was the end of it.

Even though single membership for the season could be purchased for £1 11s 6d, a sum that gave access to nets, members had a right to feel short-changed from a summer of horrid weather. Playing hours, when possible, were noon to 7pm on the first two days and 11.30am to 6pm or 6.30pm on the final day, after which hurried trips to railway stations were often required. Two such trips in 1956 saw treks from Chesterfield to Colchester, and Eastbourne to Derby. Arrival at their hotel, or their own bed, was often not until the early hours, in pre-motorway Britain; a tiring experience. It put a pressure on domestic life, as Edwin recalls.

> The players saw little of their families once the season got going. There were a few of the wives and girlfriends who were more heavily involved – Derek Morgan's wife used to sell raffle tickets and the like – but most, including Jean, liked to keep a distance from it all.

> Seen, but not heard was the motto of the time, but the reality was that

we couldn't afford it. I might have been a county cricketer with a cap, but Jean was earning more in the weaving sheds at Robinson's Mill in Chesterfield than I was! She might have come to a day here and there at Chesterfield, Derby and Ilkeston, but certainly not to away games, as she was too busy working. That was the same for all players.

In December 1956, Edwin ensured that he would see much more of Jean Burton by marrying her at Hasland Parish Church, the neighbouring village to their respective homes in Grassmoor. The service was performed by the Rector of Hasland, the Reverend C.N. Lavender, with Jean wearing a dress of white brocade with silver threads, fashioned by Jack Berry of Keighley. Edwin's brother, Arthur, was best man, with Enid Hardwick, a friend of Jean's, as bridesmaid,

Around 50 guests attended a reception at the Odeon Restaurant in Chesterfield, including Edwin's county colleagues Cliff Gladwin, Derek Hall, Alan Revill, Charlie Lee and Laurie Johnson. County coach Denis Smith was also in attendance and afterwards the couple honeymooned in London.

They made their marital home in Morley Avenue, Ashgate, near Chesterfield, although they spent the first few months of married life with Jean's parents in Grassmoor, while the property was finished. They had an opportunity to buy an old house in the village, given first refusal on it at a price of £120, but an early viewing showed that the house had no electricity and fixtures that were antiquated, even for the time.

When they finally moved in to their new home, on Good Friday, 19 April 1957, they were to stay for the next 41 years. At £2000 it proved a shrewd investment.

Wedding day, December 1, 1956.

Chapter Eight

West Indian summer

By the summer of 1957, Edwin was 23 and an established county cricketer. He had developed his skills over a six-year apprenticeship and had especially adapted them to the changes of the lbw law.

When he started his career, the batsman had to be hit on the pads in line of the stumps to be given out lbw, the ball itself having pitched there. It gave little margin for spin and the adaptation of the law, to allow an lbw decision for a ball pitching outside off stump where the batsman had played no shot, was welcomed by off spin bowlers throughout the country, as Edwin explains.

> On a good wicket, like those at Derby, I would get in close to the stumps and my bowling hand would come over middle stump. If I pitched just outside off stump, I only needed a little turn to get them out lbw, or bowled if they didn't play it right.

> If it was turning, I would bowl around the wicket, again aim just outside off stump, but allow the angle to make the batsman play and bring the short legs into the game. I had a lot of success with it, but gradually realised that I needed something more to get out the top batsmen.

That 'something more' was an arm ball, that was around five years in its creation and became regarded as among the best in the game. Later county stalwart, Alan Hill, maintains that he saw no one bowl a better arm ball than Edwin. It is more often today given the magical name of 'doosra', a term that makes Edwin laugh.

> It is an arm ball variant, nothing more, nothing less. I started working on mine in 1952, in the nets at Derby. I used to take a tin of balls and bowl it, for hour after hour. Essentially, I was turning the seam and letting the ball swing, rather than turn.

> Turn wasn't what I wanted. I was looking for a different ball from the stock off spinner. I had a top spinner as well, but that could sometimes turn a little. This arm ball had to swing and put the batsman in two minds, as well as bring the wicket-keeper and slip into play.

> I worked on it for a long time before I brought a batsman in to face it. Then I bowled it to them, mixing it with the other deliveries I had and didn't try it in a match until 1957. By that time, I reckoned that I had it perfected and could by and large put it in the right areas whenever I wanted to.

A classic example of Edwin's arm ball came against Worcestershire at

Kidderminster in 1966. His team mate of that period, Brian Jackson, takes up the story.

> Basil d'Oliveira had just returned from England duty where he had done well and was given a hero's welcome by a large crowd. He was immaculately turned out and looked full of confidence as he walked out to bat, acknowledging the crowd's applause and looking set to enjoy his spell at the crease.
>
> He took guard to Edwin as the applause died down and Edwin set his field. He was coming round the wicket, a sign that the ball was turning, something that Basil would have been very aware of.
>
> Edwin ran in, that six-step run that we knew so well. The ball pitched middle and leg and, as Basil went back to turn it with the spin through the leg side, it kept on going and flattened his off stump. He was one of the best batsmen in England – maybe the world – and had been completely deceived by Edwin's arm ball.
>
> You could have heard a pin drop as he walked slowly back to the pavilion.

The 1957 season opened on May 4 against Yorkshire at Bradford. On a cold, sunny morning, losing Charlie Lee to Fred Trueman's second ball of the season was not the most auspicious of starts. Only the ever-reliable Hamer and Alan Revill showed any form, the latter ironic as Revill was to endure a difficult summer. It saw him released by the county and moving to Leicestershire for three seasons. A popular and garrulous team mate, memorably described by Michael Parkinson as being able to 'talk the leg off an iron pot', he was particularly missed by Edwin.

> He was a lovely bloke and we spent a lot of time together. He was a good cricketer, but struggled in that final year. You would call him a selfless batsman, prepared to give his wicket away in the quest for quick runs to enable a declaration. It was as a friend that I missed him most, as well as one of the best short leg fielders I ever saw.

Derbyshire lost that opening fixture after fine batting by Brian Close and Ray Illingworth, while the irrepressible Fred Trueman took five wickets in each innings, as well as rendering George Dawkes *hors de combat* for the rest of the match with a blow on the foot, as he dismissed him lbw.

It was not a good start, but the side showed much improved form over the summer, eventually finishing fourth behind champions Surrey, Northamptonshire and a Yorkshire side that was on the way to greatness, acknowledged by Edwin.

> They had some wonderful players at that time. Ken Taylor, Frank Lowson, Brian Close and Willie Watson were all fine batsmen, while Fred Trueman was, as everyone knew, a terrific fast bowler. They had Johnny Wardle, Ray Illingworth and Close to bowl spin and it needed a very good team performance to beat them.

Such a performance was less than three weeks away. In the intervening period, Derbyshire won their next two games. Leicestershire were heavily beaten at their Aylestone Road ground, a venue not used by the county since 1939. Edwin had three for 17 in nine overs in the first innings and was nigh-unplayable in the second, with figures of 16-5-19-6. Gladwin and Jackson then demolished Essex at Burton-on-Trent, before Yorkshire visited the scenic splendours of Queens Park in Chesterfield for the season's return fixture.

The game was a benefit for Les Jackson, the first awarded by the county since the one for all-rounder Arthur Morton in 1924. Astonishing as it may now seem, a crowd of 11,000 attended the first day and Edwin recalls them being 'row after row deep' at the bandstand side of the ground. The Yorkshire bowling didn't have the edge of the previous encounter and Derbyshire amassed 292 in their first innings, led by a typically solid and understated innings by John Kelly, who made 106 and was supported down the order.

Yorkshire's opening batsmen were still together at the close and by lunch next day the visitors had reached 131 for two, with Brian Close well set, He went on to make 120 in the afternoon session, before being smartly stumped by George Dawkes off Edwin's bowling. The rest of the side folded before Gladwin and Jackson, being all out just before tea for 199, Jackson taking five for 51. After tea, Derbyshire's top order crumbled before Trueman and Bob Platt, but Donald Carr and George Dawkes launched a breathtaking counter-attack. Dawkes began by hooking Platt for six and made a run-a-minute 75.

Derbyshire were 174 for five at the close, 267 runs ahead and the question as the crowds turned up on the third day was when the declaration might come. Carr and Laurie Johnson hit freely in an unbroken stand of 85, before Carr's declaration left Yorkshire 325 to win in 260 minutes.

Jackson dismissed both openers in the first 20 minutes, but solid contributions down the order left the visitors in with a chance, before Carr's left hand slow bowling took three quick wickets. The new ball saw Jackson take wickets in his second and third overs, but another 15 were to elapse before he returned for a final spell and had Platt caught at slip by Laurie Johnson with the last ball of his 29th over. There were eight minutes to spare and he had six for 63, giving match figures of eleven wickets for 114 runs.

It had been a wonderful match and a successful one for Jackson. Gate receipts totalled £1565, with a further £227 in collections; and he went on to another golden season, taking 138 wickets at an average of 16.

So too did Cliff Gladwin, the 11th time that he had reached that landmark, but at 41 the bowler, who also passed 1500 wickets for the county during the season, realised that times were changing. Edwin explains:

Cliff had become Derbyshire's record all-time wicket-taker during the season and bowled nearly 900 overs. Yet an experimental law had been introduced, which limited the number of fielders a bowler could have on the leg side. A few of us felt that in-swing bowlers like Cliff were being targeted in an attempt to 'brighten up' cricket. He had a lot of skill, however and he was affected less than some others who were less talented.

The biggest victims were off spinners. Even on turning wickets, we were forced to have four fielders on the off side, which made no sense. You either dispensed with a backward short leg, or fine leg, meaning you missed out on wickets or conceded more runs, as you couldn't have both.

Grumbles aside, it was a fine season for the county, who were never lower than fifth in the table and were top in early June. Nevertheless, Donald Carr hinted at problems ahead in his review of the season in the club's 1958 yearbook, highlighting that only Les Jackson and Edwin had emerged from local cricket since the war to become county regulars.

The side was growing old. Besides the 41-year old Gladwin, Jackson was 36, Hamer 40, Dawkes 36, Kelly 35 and most of the others over 30. Only Edwin and Derek Morgan of the regulars had plenty of time on their side, although some of those named above would continue, with success, for several seasons.

There had been opportunities for younger players, but none had cemented their potential and talent with sustained performance at first-class level. One such player, who made his senior debut in 1957 after first joining the ground staff in 1952, was Keith Mohan. At the mention of his name, Edwin laughs:

Alan Revill gave us a few laughs over the years but perhaps the funniest of them all, often at the root of things that went on, was Keith.

One time he was told to whiten the boots of all the players before a game and all the players left theirs outside the dressing room, including Reg Carter ,who also left a pair of black plimsolls there to air. Keith duly whitened them as well!

Another time, he came across a small fire in the staff room at the County Ground and, thinking quickly, put it out with some water. He went and reported it to the club secretary, Will Taylor, thinking he'd maybe get commended, or even better, a few shillings for his trouble.

He was mistaken. Will looked at him sternly and said 'You silly so-and-so, you should have let the bugger burn. We're fully insured.'

Then there was another day, when he was late for a first team game. We were supposed to be at the ground an hour before play, but Keith slept in and only got there half an hour before the start.

His late arrival was mentioned later that night on television and in the next week or so he got seven alarm clocks sent to him by supporters in the post!

Groundsman Walter Goodyear is another with vivid memories of the player.

One day, after lunch, I told the players that I was going to move the motorised roller from its location in one of the nets so they could practice. Keith jumped up, grabbed the keys and volunteered to do it for me.

He started up the engine, then put it into what he thought was reverse gear. It wasn't. He drove forward and straight through the back of the net, taking down all of them – and they took some time to erect properly.

I went into my hut and came out with a length of rope, which I gave to him.

'Take this round the back of the pavilion and see if you can make a better job of hanging yourself,' I told him.

Edwin bowled steadily throughout the season despite the fielding restrictions. The only times he was hit was against Worcestershire, where he freely admits that brothers Peter and Dick Richardson had his measure. Taking a long stride down the wicket, the left-handers would slog-sweep against the spin, aware that Edwin couldn't reinforce the field to counteract it.

There was a five-wicket haul against champions Surrey, but Edwin was often used to contain during a summer in which Derek Morgan almost became a third wicket centurion. After several years of promise, Morgan emerged as one of the best all-rounders in the game, his seam bowling backing up the opening pair and stepping into the breach when Gladwin missed a few matches through injury.

Edwin sustained a pulled thigh muscle against Leicestershire at Chesterfield, causing him to be carried off and miss three matches. He had previously been relatively injury-free.

I was usually fine, but I did have problems with my spinning finger. Jim Laker had the same problem and we used a similar method to sort it. I developed a callus on my middle finger, but the inside of my index finger used to split. There was an old woman in our village, Mrs Hart, who had lost the tip of one of her fingers and when she heard about the problems I had, she told me to use Friar's Balsam.

I used to put it on my finger each night and it would harden the skin, so you could bowl without too much pain the next day.

There were two viewing highlights for Edwin during that summer, both of them at Chesterfield. One was watching an extraordinary century by the West Indian all-rounder, Collie Smith.

He was an astonishing player. Cliff bowled him for a duck in the first innings, but in the second he hit 133 in three hours. It was really hot and he had us chasing the ball all afternoon. He hit Cliff back over his head onto the pavilion roof and there weren't many people did that over the years. What has stayed with me was his timing - it was astonishing.

Less than three months later, the lad was killed in a car crash in Staffordshire and he was a massive loss to the game. We also faced Roy Gilchrist in that game and he was seriously fast and nasty. He had quite a temper and bowled a bouncer at Donald Carr that was in the wicket-keeper's gloves before Donald was in position to hook – and that was a shot that Donald played especially well.

Edwin also recalls from a 'special summer of cricket' the bowling out of Middlesex for 29 at Queen's Park.

It was a damp wicket and we had ground out a lead of 51 in the first innings. Cliff had taken six for 23 in 25 overs in the first innings and when they started their second he had five for five as they slipped to 11 for six by the close.

We were convinced that had we carried on that night they wouldn't have made 20. As it was, they were out for 29 the next morning and Cliff had eleven for 41 in the match.

Derbyshire won none of their last five matches, but could look back on a fine summer of cricket.

At the indoor school in Derby, demolished in March 2015:
Alan Revill, Les Jackson, Edwin Smith, Denis Smith (coach) and Brian Furniss.

Chapter Nine

Les

The weather of 1958 was almost as bad as 1956. Only two of Derbyshire's 15 home matches escaped interruption and rain affected play on 43 of the county's scheduled 90 days of cricket.

It was the last summer in county colours for Cliff Gladwin, who had turned down lucrative league offers the previous winter to have one last season. He left on a high, taking 117 wickets in the Championship at just 15 runs each. At 42 he was still a fine bowler and was to continue taking wickets in the leagues for years, but had been frustrated by those new regulations on leg side fielders, as Edwin explains.

> Cliff liked a leg slip and a backward short leg, as well as a man back on the boundary at fine leg. The changes meant he had to dispense with one of these and it annoyed him, as it did off spin bowlers, of course. Cliff liked taking wickets and he liked bowling economically, so one of those had to be affected by the new requirements.

> We were limited to five men on the on side, but I remember Bob White of Middlesex saying that he broke the rules when he bowled round the wicket, because he then had six!

The loss of Gladwin to the county was in some ways offset by the emergence of Harold Rhodes, son of the former county spinner. Having switched from spin to seam at the suggestion of Derbyshire coach Denis Smith, Harold took 71 Championship wickets at less than 19 runs each and made an immediate impression, according to Edwin.

> Harold had been around the staff for a few years and we all knew he could bowl. He had a nice run up, an easy sideways action and a very 'whippy' arm action. In due course that action would be looked at by cricket authorities from every possible angle, but there was never any thought among us that his delivery was anything other than legitimate.

> What became very clear was that Harold was quick. Genuinely quick. There were a lot of lively bowlers on the circuit, but as Frank Tyson disappeared after a meteoric career, effectively burned out on the slow Northampton wickets, Harold and Fred Trueman were comfortably the quickest in the country.

> I fielded at short leg for him occasionally and the ball would zip through consistently quickly, but when he really bent his back, which he did at least once an over, I used to feel sorry for the batsmen.

> He learned quickly from Cliff about using the new ball well. The two

of them watched Tyson bowl at our opening batsmen one day at Northampton and Frank's first ball was a bouncer, which cleared John Kelly and the wicket-keeper, then hit the sight screen after one bounce.

'Did you see that?' said Harold, to which Cliff replied 'Aye, what a ruddy waste of a new ball'.

With Derek Morgan cementing his position as a genuine all-rounder with 67 wickets at under 20, Edwin found himself playing every game but often being ignored, as wickets were more conducive to what was often a four-man seam attack.

There were only two five-wicket hauls and Edwin's lot became that of a stock bowler, either allowing the bowlers to change ends or allow them a breather on the rare occasion that one of them failed to make a breakthrough. Derbyshire were fifth in the table when the summer ended, Edwin's contribution a more modest than usual 54 wickets at 28.

> It was perhaps then that I realised that I had to work on my batting. I only averaged ten with the bat, but there were games where I bowled less than ten overs, while at one point I didn't bowl in two successive matches. Going in at ten, they weren't playing me for my batting, so I realised that I had to be able to contribute more when the conditions weren't 'right' for my bowling.

One of the games in which Edwin didn't bowl was at the old Ind Coope and Allsopps ground at Burton-on-Trent. The game ended in a single day on a green, soft wicket, the ball flying through at different heights and moving both ways for all the seam bowlers.

Batting first, Derbyshire struggled to 74 all out, with George Dawkes hitting out to make top score of 19 and Edwin unbeaten on six. Against Les Jackson and Harold Rhodes, quicker than their Hampshire counterparts, Malcolm Heath and Derek Shackleton, the visitors were in turn dismissed for just 23, Jackson taking five for 10, Rhodes four for 12. Contemporary reports note that there was 'some backing away', as the hostile pair bowled unchanged through an innings that lasted less than 17 overs.

Derbyshire's second innings began in mid-afternoon and once the effects of the roller wore off, wickets began to fall. Only a typical innings of great bravery and no little skill by Derek Morgan (46) got Derbyshire to a total of 107, leaving a victory target of 159.

Ninety minutes, plus the extra half-hour remained in the day and Derbyshire won with 17 minutes in hand. Hampshire were all out for 55 and Edwin acknowledges the captaincy of Donald Carr in the triumph.

> Their opening bowlers tired in the second innings and Derek capitalised on some loose balls as they did so in a typically gritty knock. Maybe their captain, Colin Ingleby-Mackenzie, should have changed things, but he didn't. Donald realised when Harold Rhodes was tiring in the second innings and brought on Derek, who took three for four in five overs. Les had four for 16 and nine for 26 in the match.

There were around 3,000 there, but I have had a lot more than that claimed to have been on the ground over the years!

Irrespective of the bad weather, the summer was a triumph for Les Jackson. He was 37 before the season and suffered a groin strain in the opening fixture against Oxford University. Although missing six Championship matches that year, he finished it top of the national bowling averages, with 143 wickets in all games at 10.99 each. It was the lowest average of any bowler taking a hundred wickets in the 20th century and testimony to his skill in a summer in which he cut down his pace, but still continued to move the ball at speed in either direction.

How good was he? Edwin is quick in his reply.

Les was the best. None of us would have swapped him for any other bowler in the country. Fred Trueman was quick when conditions suited him, he had a point to prove, or he had his back up; Brian Statham was quick and accurate, but Les just kept on bowling, whatever the conditions.

He wasn't lightning fast, more awkward. Harold Rhodes was much quicker, but Les seemed to arrow the ball in at the batsmen's ribs and thighs and most of them got hit at one time or another.

When Tom Graveney played against us and saw Les, he used to rub the inside of his thighs as a joke, because he had done it many times before at the crease! Ask any batsman of that era who they least like facing and Les would always be in the top three.

Yet this modest man, who was 26 before he played for the Derbyshire senior team, had none of the brashness of others on the circuit. He didn't indulge in 'verbals' and if a catch was dropped off his bowling, he was the antithesis of his colleague, Cliff Gladwin.

Les would sometimes smile, maybe clap his hands in recognition of a decent attempt and then say 'Bad luck, catch next 'un'. Nothing riled him.

There was one occasion, when we played Kent at Chesterfield, I was fielding in close for Les, as he bowled at Colin Cowdrey. The ball was fairly fizzing through and Colin, a good player of quick bowling, was really struggling against him. We all kept raising our eyebrows at one another and eventually I went over to Les between overs.

'You're going through fast today,' I said to him, hoping for the reason.

'I'm just seeing how quick I can bowl, Edwin,' was his reply. Nothing more than that, he just wanted to test himself against a very good player.

His team mates of the era attest to Les moving the ball around on the green linoleum floor of the indoor cricket school, something no one else managed to do. The shrewd soon realised that if they allowed him to get them out early, he would ease back. He liked to prove a point, to himself,

Drawing of Edwin from the Derby Telegraph.

The 'collection plate'.

if no one else.

Asked the secret of his success, he said that he merely held his fingers along the seam and 'buggered about with it until something happened'. It was an understated response typical of the man, but the feeling remains that he was poorly treated by national selectors. Even in an era of good seam bowlers, umpires and players alike rated Les up with the best. Edwin has a theory on his omission from England sides over the years.

Les was massive in the top half of his body. He had a big chest, a strong back and powerful shoulders from his time spent down the pit. Funnily enough, his bottom half looked less developed and perhaps the selectors felt that he would break down on an overseas tour. It was nonsense, because his workload over the years was substantial and he rarely let us down.

His action was not conventional either. His run up was ordinary, perhaps even awkward, no more than ten or 12 paces and it all ended in an almost round-arm 'sling' that would never have been seen in the MCC coaching manual. He was sent down to see Alf Gover at his cricket school in London, but he only suggested minor adjustments. It worked for him and us and season after season he delivered the goods

Walter Goodyear tells another story about Jackson that typifies the man.

One day he came off at the end of play and took off a cricket boot, then tossed it to me. It was full of blood.

'I had a nail come through the sole this morning Wal ... can you get it sorted for me?'

He'd bowled nearly all day with a nail sticking in his foot! Can you imagine them doing that today? I borrowed someone's bicycle and took it to a cobbler on East Street in Derby. He was just closing up, but when I told him I'd got Les Jackson's boot for repair, he opened up again and sorted it, so I could take it back to him for the next day's play.

The final word should be Edwin's. How would he sum up his former colleague?

'As an outstanding bowler, a valued team mate and a very good friend,' comes the quick reply.

Chapter Ten

A decade ends

As the 1950s drew to a close, the lot of the county cricketer had changed little.

The financial rewards were few, but the camaraderie of the circuit remained. Transport was slowly improving, the first part of the M1 motorway opening in 1959 to link Watford and Rugby, though the vagaries of fixture scheduling led to many frantic trips across country late at night. Car ownership in the UK exceeded three in ten of households, one of them now belonging to Edwin Smith.

> I'd relied on the likes of Cliff and Les to give me lifts for several years and it was nice to be able to repay some of those favours. It saved me a lot of travelling time, although there were still journeys where it was deemed more financially viable for us to go by train.

The rain of 1958 was followed by better weather in 1959 and it was a summer of firm, true wickets and regular sunshine. Perhaps it was a reflection on fortunes at Derbyshire, where young players were at last starting to emerge.

> We saw the likes of Ian Buxton, Ian Hall and Peter Eyre appear, tribute to the work done by Denis Smith. Ian hit the ball hard and swung it into batsmen, while Ian Hall became a really gritty, dogged opening batsman over the next decade. He was more valued by his team mates than perhaps by spectators and the opposition.

> He didn't play too much in front of the wicket, but Ian became a valuable and brave opening batsman, once making a century in each innings against Kent. He played fast bowling very well and they gave up bowling bouncers at him. He either ducked or swayed and could never be tempted to hook.

> Peter Eyre was a lovely player and a smashing bloke. If I could have cloned him I could take on most sides, because he would always give you a hundred per cent. Like Harold, his career was affected by controversy, as there was a suggestion that he threw. He didn't – tests later showed him to have a double-jointed elbow. He could bat as well, but he had a lot of bad luck with injuries.

> He also suffered from alopecia and was quite self-conscious about it for a while, so took to wearing a wig. One time at Ilkeston, he was running in to bowl and he'd not properly applied the adhesive tape and elastic on it. The wig was bouncing up and down as he ran in and

none of us could take our eyes off it. Eventually, he stopped bothering with one.

It was a golden summer and Derbyshire's batsmen enjoyed themselves. Donald Carr scored 2165 runs, a Championship aggregate record for Derbyshire that still stands, while Arnold Hamer, at the age of 42, scored 1850. At last Laurie Johnson fulfilled the talent that everyone knew he had, with 1480 runs, while Charlie Lee and Derek Morgan also passed four figures.

Laurie had first played in 1949, having come over from Barbados to train as a sugar engineer. He always looked a player of class, but for a long time struggled for runs on English wickets. In 1959 it all clicked, maybe because the wickets were similar to back home. He never looked back.

A lot of people think that was a long apprenticeship, but he went to what was then British Guiana for three years to work on a sugar plantation. He only played one game of cricket in those three years, so when he came back here he was pretty much starting from scratch.

What a player though! Once he got the measure of the English wickets his cover driving was typically Caribbean and very powerful, while his fielding at point was world-class. He had a bullet-like throw, which I suppose you would expect from someone who once held the junior world record for throwing a cricket ball!

The previous summer, Johnson had scored only 693 runs in 50 Championship innings, with a highest of 49 and an average of 17. Yet Denis Smith rated him and for the next six summers he became the batting linchpin, whose aggressive play brought thousands of runs.

For Edwin, the summer brought a welcome return to form. While Jackson again headed the averages with 132 wickets at 16, he had 79 at just under 27 runs each.

Lancastrian Bob Berry had been specially registered before the season. A slow left-arm bowler, he had been forced out of his native county, then Worcestershire, by a surfeit of spinners, despite having twice played for England. He flighted the ball well, but a tendency to bowl loose deliveries meant he never became established. While the intention was for he and Edwin to make up a spin bowling partnership, Berry was generally out-bowled in the matches they played together, finishing the summer with just 17 Championship wickets at 45 runs each.

Edwin bowled especially well in the win against Nottinghamshire at Trent Bridge, with match figures of six for 92 from 51 overs. Five for 67 against the touring Indian side, traditionally fine players of spin bowling, underlined his credentials, as did an analysis of five for 32 that enabled a win over Hampshire at Derby.

At Worthing, figures of six for 44 helped force another win and Edwin was now seen as a spin bowler of genuine, consistent ability. How does he remember that summer?

> I enjoyed it, though perhaps not as much as the batsmen did! Donald and Arnold were in fine form all summer and it was a pleasure to watch them both when they were in full flow. Laurie Johnson finally made the runs that he had hinted at for years and we looked a decent batting side that summer.
>
> In the middle of June we were top of the table, but then we had a bad run and seventh place was probably a fair reflection on the cricket we played.

Harold Rhodes was capped against India and on the hard wickets bowled very quickly. He looked set for a long and glittering international career, but as events were to prove, it was not to be.

Around the wicket.

Chapter Eleven

Setbacks at the start
of the Swinging Sixties

The new decade has gone down in history as one when black and white austerity turned to vibrant psychedelia. In many ways it started the world which we are familiar with. County cricket was to change dramatically too. Overseas stars would arrive, and one-day cricket to capture the public imagination. Yet as it began, Edwin, like his team mates, was working away as he always had, combining a winter of graft in whatever work was available, with a summer plying his trade.

While his county rose to fifth position in 1960, it is not a summer that Edwin remembers fondly.

As a side we did well, but we did so on the back of 1800 runs from Laurie Johnson, who was now batting as well as anyone in the country, together with 150 Championship wickets from Les. He was 39 before the season started but bowled over a thousand overs. If the skipper wanted wickets he left Les on. If he wanted to control things, he brought him back again. He bowled almost 400 overs more than any other seam bowler and went for less than two runs an over. It was a fantastic effort and he continued to be the most respected bowler on the county circuit.

Yet all was not well.

Harold Rhodes fell victim to the throwing 'witch hunt' and was no-balled in two different matches, one of them against the South Africans. That was ironic, because Geoff Griffin, who everyone knew threw the ball, bowled almost the same number of overs in the game without question.

It was the start of a very tough few seasons for Harold, throughout which he showed great dignity and professionalism as he sought to clear his name. He underwent many filming sessions and he was watched from every conceivable angle. The reality was that it was impossible for him to throw the ball, because of his classic, sideways action. The ones who were throwing did so from an open-chested action, much like a player at a dart board.

Denis Smith was a very good coach and neither he, Cliff or Les had ever expressed any concerns over the way Harold bowled.

Arnold Hamer and John Kelly left the staff that summer. Hamer was 43 and missed much of it with a broken thumb, after being hit by South

African paceman Neil Adcock. Kelly was five years his junior, but had only two Championship innings in 1960, as Charlie Lee and Ian Hall took the opening berths. It wasn't an ideal pairing, as Edwin explains.

Charlie and Ian were good players, but as opening batsmen they were very alike. Charlie could play shots, but got bogged down at times and with Ian a dour player as his partner, we were very slow at the start of the innings. Both were good players of quick bowling but bowlers imposed shackles that we struggled to shake off subsequently.

Arnold and John had complemented each other so well. Bowlers knew that if they over-pitched early in an innings Arnold would be after them. He was powerful and put his full body into shots, while John was more wristy. When he got going, John was perhaps the best-looking batsman in the side. Arnold was never stylish, but he was a very fine player. His cover driving was enjoyed by everyone, except those bowling to him and had he not lost those years to the war, he could have played for England, without a doubt.

Yorkshire lost a few players to other counties over the years and he was as good as any of them.

Despite his age, Hamer was apparently 'devastated' at the decision to release him, according to Walter Goodyear, who tried to console the player after coming across him when the news had been broken to him. One more season, perhaps partnering the young Hall and encouraging a more positive approach, may have been worthwhile, but the county's perennially parlous finances meant that economies had to be made.

Will Taylor, the county's secretary from 1908 to 1959, had been replaced by Major Douglas Carr, the brother of the Derbyshire captain. Both men had a difficult job in balancing the books at a county where membership was traditionally low and money in short supply, as former groundsman Walter Goodyear recalled.

Mr Taylor treated the club's money as if it was his own, which in many ways it was, of course. There was rarely any spare cash for ground improvements and for most of my time at the club I had to ask favours of people to get tarmac, grass seed, fertiliser and other materials.

I came to know that the time to ask for money was when he had people with him, as he didn't want to appear 'tight'. We had a few run-ins over the years, but he left the club in a better financial state than he found it, as well as overseeing a period of considerable success.

The summer of 1960 was the club's first without Will Taylor at the helm for over half a century, although he was to remain involved in the club in various capacities until 1972. Edwin remembers him with fondness.

He was an outstanding administrator and learned early on that the only way the club could keep afloat was by prudent use of limited resources.

Funnily enough, he was a generous man in other ways. When my wife and I married, Will bought us a beautiful art deco alarm clock. We still have it and it still works, even after all those early morning wake-up calls!

From a playing viewpoint, the first summer of the 'golden decade' was a frustrating one for Edwin. While he made the second half century of his career against Sussex at Hove, he took only 24 wickets before a broken wrist ended his season in mid-June. This allowed Bob Berry the role of lead spinner and he responded well to the challenge, taking 60 wickets at a shade under 26 runs each. The injury was doubly unfortunate, in its timing and the way it happened.

> I was washing my car and tripped over a kerb. I landed heavily on my left hand and put a cold bandage on it immediately. The following day, I was due to play for the second team against Lancashire at St Helens and had arranged to pick up Peter Eyre on the way. My hand and wrist were so painful that Peter had to take over behind the wheel.

> When we got to the ground, I was sent immediately for an x-ray, which showed that I had broken the scaphoid bone. Denis Smith wasn't happy, as he had to drive back to Buxton for a replacement player! I was in plaster for several weeks and out for the rest of the summer.

> Later that year, in the November, I went to Lilleshall to do my advanced coaching badge and the hand was still painful. It was suggested that I get it x-rayed again, which showed that it hadn't healed. So I was in plaster for another four months, which took me up to pre-season of 1961, by the time it came off.

> Fortunately I was insured against injury and it paid me ten pounds a week during the remainder of the season, while the sick or 'club' money from the pit meant that we were perhaps better off than usual.

As he recovered at home in Grassmoor, Edwin knew that there was a challenge to his place as senior spinner in the side, but wasn't unduly worried.

> Bob was a lovely lad and a decent bowler, but he relied on flight and didn't spin the ball that much. He didn't bat either, so I was confident that once I was back to fitness I could fight off the challenge.

> Although he had played for England, I don't think he was technically as good a bowler as Reg Carter. If we had been able to retain his services, Reg could have been a good foil for me over many years.

As the 1961 season began, Edwin had spent around six of the previous nine months with his left hand and arm in plaster. While his scaphoid, the largest of the carpal bones in the wrist, was thankfully mended, the enforced inactivity left him not quite the bowler he had been.

His county did reasonably well, finishing seventh in the table, but for Edwin it was a summer of frustration. In the club's yearbook for the following year, Donald Carr commented that 'Smith only rarely troubled batsmen on good wickets'. The economy rate was still good, but there were only 46 wickets that summer and they cost over 30 runs each for the first time.

Wickets were now covered and that made life more difficult for spin bowlers across the country, but Edwin adapted and eventually became a better bowler on good wickets than when the ball was turning appreciably.

> I didn't feel right that summer. Maybe my action had changed slightly and unwittingly because of the injury. I always bowled with my left palm facing upwards as my arm came over – Arnold Hamer used to say I had the collection plate ready – and perhaps a small technicality affected the mechanics of the action.

> It is easy to overlook the mental side of a break to a cricketer too. You wonder if the first hard hit that you stop will break it again. The truth is that a broken bone mends and is perhaps stronger than it was before, of course, but for whatever reason I didn't bowl at my best in 1961.

> Yet I thought about my game and started to use more flight, the arm ball and a top spinner. I got in closer to the stumps, so my arm was coming over middle stump. If I held on my front foot as I bowled, I got more turn, so sometimes I 'went through' on it, which opened up lbw decisions if the batsman missed, as it didn't turn so much.

At least Edwin's batting improved, with a career-highest aggregate of 443, at an average of just under 15. It kept him ahead of the competition, as Bob Berry failed to take advantage of the dip in form, taking only 17 wickets in his appearances.

Four batsmen passed a thousand runs, with the now-prolific Laurie Johnson highest in both aggregate and average, The dependable Charlie Lee, Yorkshireman Billy Oates and Donald Carr all did well, while in the bowling ranks Harold Rhodes reached a hundred Championship wickets for the first time, Meanwhile, Les Jackson was recalled to the England side after a 12-year gap, playing against the Australian tourists at Headingley. His Derbyshire team-mates were thrilled for the player, but also saddened, as Edwin explains.

> Les was 40 and while still a fine bowler, was understandably not quite as good as he had been. He took four for 83 in the match and went for two an over.

> Throughout the 1950s, every time the Australians came on tour they expected him to be in the England side and were astonished when it didn't happen. They knew, like everyone on the circuit did, that he was the best, most consistent seam bowler in the county game. Indeed, Donald Bradman thought him the best young quick bowler they faced as early as 1948.

> He played his part in an England win then they dropped him again, for Jack Flavell of Worcestershire. He was a good bowler, but not as good as Les. It was frustrating for all of us, but Les just got on with his game.

It was a season that suggested the end of an era, as news broke that Donald

Derbyshire at the Oval 1961. Back: Ray Swallow, David Millner, Bob Taylor, Harold Rhodes, Ian Buxton, Billy Oates. Front: Laurie Johnson, Les Jackson, Charlie Lee (captain) Derek Morgan, Edwin Smith.

Derbyshire staff in 1961. Back: Bob Berry, Billy Oates, Gordon Beet, Ray Swallow, Ian Hall, Bob Taylor. Middle row: Gilbert Ryde (scorer), David Millner, Harold Rhodes, Denis Smith (coach), Peter Eyre, Ian Buxton, Sam Weaver (physio). Front: Charlie Lee, Derek Morgan, George Dawkes, Donald Carr, Les Jackson, Edwin Smith, Laurie Johnson.

Carr was to become Assistant Secretary of the MCC from October 1962. The following summer was to be his last, while George Dawkes missed a number of matches due to a cartilage injury sustained in a car accident and was replaced by a Staffordshire lad by the name of Bob Taylor.

> Cliff Gladwin spotted Bob playing in the North Staffordshire League and recommended him to the county. In July 1960, Will Taylor went to watch him play for Staffordshire with the club chairman, Robin Buckston and he duly joined us, taking over from George when he was injured.

> It was immediately obvious that he had great hands and he was undemonstrative behind the stumps, with excellent footwork.

Over the next ten years, the Smith-Taylor partnership was to prove highly effective for the county, both in wicket-taking and as a source of valuable, late-order runs. How would Edwin compare the two wicket-keepers who spanned his first-class career?

> They were both very fine players. George was a lovely man who gave great service to Derbyshire. He had a good pair of hands and he could hit a ball very hard on his day, definitely the better batsman of the two. He had a great sense of humour as well.

> One time we played Yorkshire at Hull and I bowled what George thought was my arm ball but it pitched, then turned sharply, beating him and going down to the boundary for four byes

> Then we heard a voice from the Yorkshire contingent.

> 'Hey George. Do'st tha want a brick wall built, lad?'

> We laughed at that one for some time! There was another occasion when George chased a ball down to the boundary in his pads and dived to stop it, just inside the rope. His momentum carried him into spectators, scattering deck chairs and picnic baskets. While everyone, players included, laughed at him lying on his back with his arms and legs flailing, the batsmen ran five!

> He was a solid wicket-keeper, but Bob was simply different class. From his first game he looked like he belonged at the highest level. It's just a pity that his batting didn't come on as we hoped, as he was a tidy player who might have flourished in a better batting side. From a personal point of view, he read my arm ball better than George and his work made all the bowlers look better over the years.

> I was lucky to bowl with two such fine players and men behind the stumps.

Dawkes was to retire in 1962, confident himself that an excellent replacement had been found.

Chapter Twelve
Family man

At the end of 1962, Edwin could afford to sit back with a self-satisfied smile. He was now a proud father, Jean having given birth to a daughter, Diane, on 19 October 1961. Meanwhile his cricket career was firmly back on track, after a season in which Derbyshire had maintained seventh place. It could have been better, but poor catching let them down on occasions and Harold Rhodes suffered a troublesome groin injury that ruled him out of several matches.

Fate ruled that most of the key matches, against sides near the top of the table, took place during this time and the side was found wanting. Once again the bowling was carried by Les Jackson, in what was to prove his penultimate season. The pace may not have been that of his pomp, nor would anyone have expected it at the age of 41, but he bowled over a thousand overs and took 105 Championship wickets at a shade under 20 runs each.

With Ian Buxton proving less effective with the ball and William Richardson's availability sporadic, the seamer was both shock and stock bowler, completing over 200 more overs than Derek Morgan, who gave willing and able support.

Bob Berry left the staff at the end of the year, having rarely featured. He finished with 97 wickets at a shade under 30 over four seasons. It was perhaps not a true reflection of his talent and his figures for his third county did not compare favourably with those achieved at Lancashire and Worcestershire. It is also a worthy comparator of what Edwin's tally may have been at a county where wickets were more conducive to his skills.

There was little wrong with the batting, seven players passing a thousand Championship runs, but the injuries meant that a side accustomed to forcing positive results if they managed enough runs struggled to do so.

Edwin took 62 wickets at 22 runs each in 1962, returning to his parsimonious best in so doing. It was his job, as he explains.

> Now that wickets were covered, the number of real turners were reduced. When conditions were in my favour I was expected to get people out, but when they weren't, my role was to make the batsmen work for runs. I was 28 years old, knew my game and had to take a senior role in the side.

For the first time, Edwin passed 500 Championship runs and in the process moved up to seven in the batting order at times. He made a career-best

Edwin arrives at Derby for pre-season training, 1962.

Bowling in the nets, 1962.

70 against Hampshire at Portsmouth, hitting eleven fours in 90 minutes of batting. This was beaten at Ilkeston, when, coming in at 147 for five against Nottinghamshire, he hit 90 in just over two hours, with 16 fours among his shots. He followed this with a spell of 31 overs in which he conceded only 32 runs and took two wickets. Edwin is honest about his batting over the years.

> I was never a good player of fast bowling. I suppose it's like the old saying that's been attributed to a few people over the years – nobody likes it, but some show it more than others. I didn't make many runs against genuine quicks, though I got better at stopping in against them as I gained experience.

> I was fine against spin, though. Denis Smith always used to say 'You bowl it, you should be able to play it.'

At Buxton his economy reached new heights. Colin Milburn made 102 for Northamptonshire, his maiden century in first-class cricket, but Edwin returned the extraordinary second innings figures of 25.3-18-13-2. While Jackson and Morgan took four wickets each at the other end, they were appreciative of the control offered by Edwin. It had built pressure that ultimately proved too much for the visitors.

Similar economy was achieved against Glamorgan at Swansea, where he took four for 16 in 21 overs, at one point bowling nine successive maidens. Back on home turf at Chesterfield, figures of three for 23 in 20 overs helped to bowl out Middlesex for an easy win.

There was a wicket to be proud of, at least in later years, in June of that year, when Bob Taylor held a catch off Edwin's bowling to dismiss a young opening batsman named Geoffrey Boycott. He was playing his second first-class match and Edwin went on to the excellent figures of 34-17-39-5 against a strong Yorkshire batting side.

These were the figures of a fine bowler and the words of Donald Carr in the following year's club year book reflected his value to the side.

> Apart from Jackson and Rhodes, the main bowling success was Edwin Smith. In recent years, on good batting wickets, he had failed to trouble the batsmen, but he is now learning the 'art' of bowling and is no longer the automatic purveyor of off spin that he was previously

> He has taken a long time to learn, but I see little reason why he should not progress to considerably greater heights.

At this stage of his career, Edwin was not yet in what would normally be considered the prime of a spin bowler, yet had a decade of county experience. He had coped with changes to the covering of wickets, to the lbw law and to restrictions in the number of leg side fielders. He had learned to switch from being an attacking bowler to one whose role was to keep things quiet, then back again. He had developed new deliveries, and his batting, rising from eleven in the order to seven or eight.

Edwin had done well in his apprenticeship and in the seasons ahead would be seen as one of the best spin bowlers in the county game. He also looked forward to a new development in the form of a one-day knock-out competition in 1963, which was eventually sponsored by Gillette and bore their name.

In preparation for this, Derbyshire, Leicestershire, Nottinghamshire and Northamptonshire took part in the Midland Counties Knock-out Competition. It was the idea of Mike Turner, the Leicestershire secretary and was played to the proposed new rules, each innings limited to 65 overs with a maximum of 15 per bowler.

In the first round (or semi-final), Derbyshire played Leicestershire at Grace Road on 3 May 1962. Donald Carr won the toss and elected to bowl, Les Jackson and Harold Rhodes opening the bowling. It was a good batting wicket and the home side scored 250 for five in their allotted overs, Maurice Hallam top-scoring with 86. Rhodes had the best bowling figures, one for 39, but Edwin wasn't far behind, taking one for 43 as both bowled the maximum 15 overs.

In reply, Donald Carr and Charlie Lee reached a century partnership in 20 overs, but wickets fell and Derbyshire ended up seven runs short with more than three overs in hand. It was deemed a useful exercise, however and one that suggested the side may be competitive in the new competition.

The Gillette Cup was to prove the best and most popular of one-day competitions. Gradually, most sides realised that a quality spin bowler was always going to be an asset. Lancashire became one of the finest one-day sides with the use of 'Flat' Jack Simmons and David Hughes. Derek Underwood did well for Kent, Norman Gifford for Worcestershire, Ray East for Essex – the list is long and impressive. Leicestershire had a fine one-day side that utilised both Ray Illingworth and Jack Birkenshaw, while Peter Sainsbury and Fred Titmus proved themselves for Hampshire and Middlesex respectively.

When the John Player League started in 1969, Brian Langford of Somerset, a similar off spin bowler to Edwin, bowled his eight-over allocation against Essex at Yeovil without conceding a run.

Meanwhile Derbyshire, with one of the acknowledged best spin bowlers in the country on their staff, decided that they would go with an all-seam attack in one-day cricket for most of the period between 1963 and 1971.

During that time, Edwin Smith played just eight one-day games in nine seasons.

Even at this distance, the decision seems a strange one. Of those eight games, Edwin didn't bowl in four of them, making the team selection even stranger. Did he ever ask why he was consistently omitted?

> Once or twice, but at that time you largely accepted it and got on with things. There were many matches where perhaps even the change of pace that I would have offered may have brought dividends. I was by that stage a decent lower-order batsman and by no means the worst

fielder on the staff.

For some reason Derek Morgan, who was skipper between 1965 and 1969, chose not to play me. He was a fine player but not so good as a captain, in my opinion. Nor was Ian Buxton, who replaced him. Perhaps I was spoiled under Guy Willatt and Donald Carr ...

Had Edwin played more one-day cricket, what would have been his game plan?

I would have bowled a full length from around the wicket and aimed at leg and middle. They would have had to take me on and cleared my long on, or swept me, when my mid wicket and deep square leg would come into play and there was a danger of leg before wicket, of course, if they missed.

I'd have just bowled normal flight – no firing it in, just trying to beat them in the flight and hopefully getting them into bother if it turned. You see, most spinners today just roll it. When I started and throughout my career, you used to see spinners really tweak it between their fingers, the purchase affecting the amount of turn, of course.

I didn't try to turn every ball, but batsmen knew that I could turn it sharply and sometimes the thought of that was all it needed.

Chapter Thirteen

Bottom

The last conscripted men left the British armed forces in May 1963, something that was noted with interest by Edwin Smith as he prepared for another county season at his home in Ashgate.

He had signed up with the RAF at 18, but his job as a mechanic at Grassmoor Colliery meant that he was not called up for service, the occupation being on the exempt list. Edwin's status as a collier meant that he missed out on a potential tour in the 1950s, as he explains.

> I was told that I was in the frame for an England 'B' tour and of course the thought was very exciting, but Will Taylor, the Derbyshire secretary, told me that I couldn't go.
>
> He explained that if I did, my exemption from military service would cease and I would then effectively be lost to the county for two years. The service period was extended in October 1950, due to Britain's involvement in the Korean War.
>
> It was funny, whenever we played the RAF during that time, their captain. Alan Shirreff, used to come and ask me when I was going to join up and play with them. They had a strong side in the 1950s, with players like Peter Parfitt and Fred Trueman, but my work in the mines kept me out of their clutches, even though I missed out on a tour as a consequence.

Cricketers, like all travellers, rejoiced in the introduction of more motorways, with the first sections of the M2, M4 and M6 opening during the year. The journeys to away games would still be long, but as the decade progressed it became appreciably easier and quicker.

Once the action began, 1963 was a terrible summer for Derbyshire, who sank to bottom of the County Championship, with only two wins all summer. It was the first without Donald Carr, whose return in August for a few matches merely reinforced what was being missed. It was also the last for Les Jackson.

The latter signed off with 69 Championship wickets, but was no longer able to run through sides as in his glory days. Once again injuries to other seam bowlers left him with a heavy workload and both Harold Rhodes and Derek Morgan missed a number of matches. A bonus was the emergence of Brian Jackson from the leagues, who quickly looked at home in the first-class game and became a fine bowler for several seasons. Edwin rated him highly.

Brian was a very fine bowler. He was no relation to Les, even if a few people around the country thought he was his son! John Arlott described him as bowling a 'grudging length' and he was an aggressive bowler. With his high, whirlwind action and decent pace he became an admirable foil for Harold and there were few better opening pairs in the country over the following seasons.

He was another spotted by Cliff Gladwin in the North Staffordshire League and he took a lot of wickets for Derbyshire over the following seasons.

Skipper Charlie Lee identified the batting as the source of the problems and only three players passed the thousand run mark, the highest average being only 29. It was a transitional year and a very poor one, as Edwin explains.

Brian did well, but we realised in 1963 how important Les had been. So many times he took out the top order, had a breather, then came back to demolish the tail. When Cliff Gladwin retired, if anything Les got better.

He would just bowl and bowl. One day he took his boots off at the end of the day and one of his socks was covered in blood. He explained that it was a nasty blister that had burst, but when the captain said he should have told him about it, Les just replied 'You asked me to bowl, skipper, so I bowled.'

In the match against the West Indies in 1963 at Chesterfield, I dropped Garfield Sobers at mid on, a fairly easy chance when Les was bowling. He just shrugged his shoulders and bowled him later in the same over. Nothing ever worried him.

If you combine his stamina, accuracy and hostility over a long career, I don't think I have ever seen a better bowler. He wasn't orthodox and his action wasn't something you would teach a young player, but he was so effective.

It was one of those years. We had lost Cliff Gladwin, Les Jackson, Arnold Hamer, Donald Carr, George Dawkes and John Kelly in five seasons and you just don't replace that quality and experience overnight.

Edwin suffered from the general malaise but scored a career-best 664 runs that summer at an average of just over 16. His 38 Championship wickets were not a true reflection of the way that he had bowled; several match reports refer to him 'bowling without luck'.

In the Gillette Cup, Derbyshire started with a narrow first round win over Hampshire at Bournemouth, by six runs. Having won the toss, the home side sent Derbyshire in and with Ian Hall making 61 and Derek Morgan an unbeaten 59 they totalled 250 all out in their 65 overs.

Good fielding effected four run outs in the reply, although Mike Barnard, batting at three, anchored the innings with 98. While Les Jackson's 15 overs went for just 24 runs, Edwin bowled at the end of the innings and was entrusted with the final over.

After the first two balls went for a single and bye respectively, Barnard was bowled by Edwin, who finished with 12.3-1-60-1.

The second round tie was against Lancashire at Old Trafford and a weakened side, missing Lee, Carr, Morgan and Richardson struggled to 148 all out. Edwin's 28, batting at six, helped a recovery from a poor start, but the total looked insufficient.

While Jackson bowled his 12 overs for just 22 runs, Edwin bowled 15, conceding only 46 runs, as Lancashire eased to victory with 15 overs to spare.

At the end of the summer the Derbyshire chairman, Robin Buckston, agreed with Denis Smith that Edwin should spend a fortnight in Essex over the winter. England all-rounder Trevor Bailey had a cricket school there and it was felt that it would be a beneficial move. Edwin takes up the story.

> I went down there and bowled for a couple of days while Trevor watched. We chatted about cricket and my approach to the game and then he told me that he couldn't do anything for me!

> He said that I had just had one of those seasons that all players have at times. You're not in especially bad form, but the ball just misses the stumps or the outstretched hand and your figures suffer accordingly.

> What I did do was spend time working on my batting, which had a very positive impact in 1964.

There were disappointments for Edwin before the following summer. Skipper Charlie Lee retired to concentrate on his teaching career, leaving Edwin and Derek Morgan the last of the 1950s side. While not unexpected, Lee being 40, it left a void in the dressing room.

> Charlie was the first professional captain at Derbyshire since 1889 and he did a decent job with a much weaker team than those skippered by Guy Willatt and Donald Carr.

> He had an awful start at Derbyshire and played his first season with a broken leg that hadn't healed properly. After that he became a solid batsman, although it would be hard to say that his opening partnerships with Ian Hall were exciting. Occasionally, perhaps just to show that he could, he would play a few shots, but Charlie valued his wicket and protected it fiercely. He was a fighter, a very good man to have on your side.

> He was a lovely man, with a great sense of humour. One time at Northampton, when it was a typically sandy wicket, prepared for their spin bowlers, he suggested that a sign should be erected, saying 'Unfit for bathing'.

Another frustration was the decision to engage Micky Allen from Northamptonshire, the latest in the line of slow left-armers who were supposedly to bowl in tandem with Edwin. Once again, it was doomed to failure.

Mick was another nice lad and he had some good figures for Northamptonshire, but a few of us felt that in recruiting him the club had not looked at the bigger picture.

In bowling at Northampton, always helpful surfaces for a spinner, he had a better chance than most to impress, He also had George Tribe and Jack Manning to bowl with, so batsmen tended to have a go at him to try and break free, in much the same way that the rest of us benefited from Les and Cliff at Derbyshire.

When Tribe and Manning retired, his figures declined, yet we signed him. It was a strange move and didn't work out for him.

Two players engaged that winter were John Harvey and Mike Page, who would become regular team mates.

John was a good batsman and a very fine fielder in the covers. He was from Cambridge and fitted into the side really well for a good few summers.

Mike was a Lancashire lad, from Blackpool and became a really good player. His soft hands made him a fine player of spin bowling and he usually did well against Leicestershire, where they had four spinners and the wickets were prepared to suit them.

He was also a brilliant fielder close to the wicket and held a lot of catches off me, but everyone who played with him will remember Mike as being a lot of fun.

He used to imitate Harold Bird when he umpired our games and it would get him quite agitated. You were never quite sure what Mike would do next.

He was playing a second team game one day and had been having a bit of banter with Lancashire's wicket-keeper, Keith Goodwin, who he knew very well. During the tea interval, Mike persuaded one of our seamers, Michael Glenn, to bowl a tomato to Keith, first ball after tea.

He duly bowled a full toss and Keith hit it, bang in the middle of the bat and was showered in tomato seeds!

Perhaps the biggest frustration for Edwin was the decision to overlook him for a testimonial the following summer, instead awarding one to Laurie Johnson in 1965.

I always got on very well with Laurie, who was a lovely bloke and a very good cricketer. He had played in 1949 and had a few matches in 1950, but then didn't play for the county again until 1955.

I had played constantly since 1951 and had more years on the staff than him. I had been capped in 1954, whereas he wasn't until 1958. The excuse I was given was that the decision was based on seniority and that he wouldn't be around for a second benefit, while I probably would.

My testimonial year was 1966, after 15 years at the club. Had I been given it in 1964, I would have been entitled to another when I left for good in 1974. Given that we were never well paid, it left me feeling a little undervalued, to say the least.

In 1964, Derbyshire climbed off the bottom of the table, finishing in 12th. It was a strange season, in which the county fielded a somewhat modest pace attack compared to past standards.

Brian Jackson toiled away manfully and finished top of the averages among the regular bowlers, while Derek Morgan lent solid support in bowling more overs than anyone else. The all-rounder also contributed 1600 Championship runs in a fine personal season, as well as holding the most catches among the outfielders. Edwin felt he was among the best in the country.

Time after time he came to the rescue with bat and ball. The physical demands of batting at number five and bowling first change are considerable, but Derek didn't miss a match all summer and maintained a very high standard. He was an obvious choice to take over as captain for 1965.

Charlie Lee struggled in his final summer, but Johnson, Hall and Buxton passed a thousand runs and Mike Page showed early signs of the talent that was to see him mentioned as an England possible.

The biggest concern was over Harold Rhodes. Several years of scrutiny seemed to have had an impact on the fast bowler and the new front foot ruling for no balls proved a problem for him to overcome. He missed around a third of the summer through illness and injury, looking some way removed from the England hopeful of a few seasons before. He took only 46 wickets and the side missed the penetration that he had previously offered.

As for Edwin, the summer was one in which he showed true all-round capabilities. He contributed 722 Championship runs at an average of just under 19, as well as taking 58 wickets.

As so often he did well against Yorkshire, taking two for 50 in a 30-over spell, while his efforts against the touring Australians were exemplary. In the first innings he had figures of 25-12-34-1 and in the second he had 25-5-67-4, almost bowling the county to an unlikely win after a high-scoring game.

His season best came against Nottinghamshire at Ilkeston. After Johnson's imperious century enabled the home side to make 277, a good team effort enabled a first innings lead of 84. A declaration on the final morning left the visitors a target of 279 to win in four hours, but they never got close. Edwin took five of the first six wickets and finished with the remarkable figures of 32-23-25-6.

Mick Allen played in half of the Championship matches but finished the season with only 28 wickets. Importantly he conceded around three runs per over, Edwin only two, while the latter's batting saw him regularly at seven or eight in the order.

There was only one half century, but sufficient cameos of value to justify and confirm the work that he had put in with Trevor Bailey over the winter. There was definitely something to build on in 1965.

Derbyshire staff 1964. Back: John Harvey, Chris Marks, Phil Russell, John Eyre, Mike Page, David Smith, Mick Allen.
Centre: Brian Jackson, Alan Ward, Denis Smith (coach), Peter Eyre, Maurice Hill, Ian Buxton, Sam Weaver (physio). Front: Bob Taylor, Harold Rhodes, Edwin Smith, Derek Morgan, Major Douglas Carr (secretary), Laurie Johnson, Ian Hall.

Chapter Fourteen
Summer of drama

In 1965 'Swinging London' got into full spate and for Derbyshire's seam bowlers the ball swung just as much, but a wretchedly wet summer and the controversy over Harold Rhodes made the cricket almost an afterthought.

A campaign to stamp out throwing from the game had gathered pace after the MCC tour of Australia in 1958-59, when the actions of several Australian bowlers had come under scrutiny. Seven umpires had found fault in the action of the South African, Geoff Griffin, on their 1960 tour of England, but while he bowled 29 overs without complaint against Derbyshire on that tour, umpire Paul Gibb no-balled Rhodes three times on the first evening and a further three times on the second day. Gibb felt that there was something different about Rhodes' action and, as the law was at that time, he was entitled to call him.

Those six no-balls effectively ruled the bowler out of Test cricket. The English authorities, keen to lead on stamping out throwing elsewhere, had to be seen to be putting their own house in order and Harold Rhodes effectively became their sacrificial lamb.

The Derbyshire players, like Rhodes, became accustomed to repeated filming and the studying of the bowler's action from all angles. At one stage he had been filmed wearing a splint on his elbow and changed to a more slinging action with the arm behind his back, a similar style to that used by Les Jackson. While the cloud still hung over the player, his struggle for form, especially in 1964, meant that no one complained. Rhodes himself admitted having a 'whippy' wrist action, but there was nothing illegal in that.

Fred Trueman wrote the foreword for Rhodes' later autobiography and contrasted the bowler's classic sideways-on action with that of acknowledged 'chuckers', where the leading foot generally splayed out towards cover and gulley and not down the pitch in the orthodox manner.

Everything changed in 1965. It was a bowler's summer and in Harold Rhodes and Brian Jackson, Derbyshire had the two most successful bowlers in the country. By the end of the season, Rhodes had taken 119 Championship wickets at 11; Jackson 120 at just over 12. Logic dictated that while a call to international cricket was unlikely for the latter at 33, at 29 Rhodes was perhaps in his physical prime. There were suggestions of a recall in the media, as his early season form was excellent. A winter tour to Australia would need a strong pace attack and on form there was no one better than Harold Rhodes.

He had figures of seven for 38 as Derbyshire nearly beat Warwickshire in the Championship and the side turned up at Lord's for their second round Gillette Cup match at Lord's against Middlesex after an easy win over Oxford University, where Edwin had five wickets for 23 runs. Edwin was twelfth man for the one-day game but remembers the ill-feeling clearly.

> We bowled well to put them out for 161, but after a good start, we had collapsed to 77 for eight. Then Bob Taylor and Harold added 74 for the ninth wicket and it came down to needing 11 off the last three balls.

> At that point Ted Clark fired all three well down the leg side, presumably on the instruction of his captain, Fred Titmus. Such a ball was not deemed a wide at that time, but it just wasn't the sort of thing that you did. It made for an acrimonious end to a good match and was unnecessary.

> Just over a fortnight later, Middlesex were due at Chesterfield for a Championship match. Apparently one or two of their players had discussed a protest about Harold's bowling, even to the point of insisting that he was left out of the team.

It didn't come to that and Rhodes replied with figures of six for 24 as Middlesex were bowled for 85 and Derbyshire went on to win with ease. After it, Fred Titmus reported Rhodes to Lord's, although the two umpires, Tom Spencer and Hugo Yarnold, had been satisfied with his bowling.

Worse was to follow. Rhodes had been filmed during the Gillette Cup match at Lord's and based on that film the MCC felt his action still suspect. Doug Insole, chairman of the Test selectors, wrote to Derbyshire and said that he couldn't be selected for the England team. No action was taken against Titmus for his comments.

When the South Africans arrived at Queen's Park on 26 June, Rhodes was top of the national bowling averages and the press clamour for his inclusion in the national team grew to a crescendo. Edwin takes up the story.

> It was the first tour match for them and a dull, cloudy day. Eddie Barlow, who later came to Derbyshire, got 50, but only Graeme Pollock and Colin Bland got going among the rest and they were all out for 149. Harold took four for 35 and bowled very well.

> We had been batting poorly and did so for most of the season, to be fair. After reaching 75 without loss, we were all out for 143.

> In the first innings, Jack Crapp had umpired at square leg for Harold, but when they began their second innings, Sid Buller was in that position as he began the second over. After the first ball he moved to point, where he watched the next two, then moved back to square leg, where he no-balled the next two deliveries. Harold finished the over bowling slow leg breaks off a short run.

Derbyshire won the match by seven wickets, their first victory over a full-strength touring side since beating New Zealand in 1937. Edwin bowled beautifully in the match, returning figures of 23-1-43-2 and 19.4-11-29-2. With Colin Bland, Graeme Pollock and the South African captain Peter Van der Merwe among his wickets, he had coped well with the best, but remembers the match more for its atmosphere after Buller's actions

> It was poisonous, dark. Sid was a good man and a respected umpire, but he got dreadful abuse from the crowd, who slow hand-clapped him as he walked off at tea, accompanied by two policemen. There was one old chap there who hooked him round his neck with a walking stick. It was very quiet in the dressing room. Harold was devastated, we all were for him.

Mike Page was standing at square-leg, alongside Buller, when Rhodes was called and couldn't believe it.

> There was nothing wrong with Harold's action. We never once questioned it among the team and when Sid called no ball, my first thought was that we had too many men behind square. We all gradually realised what had happened and it was awful – and totally wrong.

Neither the players nor supporters could understand how, after three and a half years and the scrutiny of 29 umpires, including Buller, Harold Rhodes was suddenly being called for throwing again. There were suggestions that it was a move to save the selectors from embarrassment, what Ian Wooldridge in the Daily Mail called a 'ceremonial calling ... no spur of the moment decision'. It was something firmly believed by the players, according to Edwin.

> What rankled was the fact that they did it now, when he was taking wickets. There was something different about Harold's action and it was later proven to be a hyper-extension of the elbow. In other words, it went past straight, in the latter part of his delivery swing, by around ten degrees. To the naked eye, it perhaps sometimes gave the illusion of a throw, but anyone who understood the mechanics of bowling should have realised that it is almost impossible to throw from a sideways position.

> Besides anything else, Harold was relentlessly accurate, something that 'chuckers' could never achieve.

Perhaps the player's success was at the root of it all and those spoken to by the author still feel that the catalyst for events were the two games against Middlesex. One told of another player who had a very short first-class career when his action came under scrutiny.

> There was a spinner at Somerset, David Doughty, who was widely reckoned to throw in a brief career. In a game against Kent, the umpires decided he should be removed from the attack at the same time that Colin Cowdrey came to the crease. He asked why they were taking him off and was told that they thought he was throwing.

> 'Leave him on' said Cowdrey, 'He's not throwing very well!'

The players were without exception supportive, although events spawned black humour, Rhodes being nicknamed 'Percy' after the television gardener, Percy Thrower. He was not the only one under scrutiny in a difficult summer, as Edwin explains.

> Peter Eyre was another whose action was questioned. He had to change his action but they eventually discovered that he was double-jointed. It was a witch hunt and how Harold managed to conduct himself with such dignity over the years was a mystery to us all. It spoke volumes of the man really. He should have been an England regular and many worse bowlers opened the bowling for England over the years.

Edwin was another who was being mentioned in higher circles and in the press. With Mick Allen unable to bowl with the requisite accuracy and taking only 22 wickets, Edwin's 71 at just under 20 were appreciated by his captain, who said that Edwin 'bowled his off spin magnificently, with no little skill and great stamina'.

For the latter comment he was perhaps thinking of the summer's drawn final match at Scarborough. Early on the second morning, Derbyshire having been bowled for 112 on the first, Rhodes tore muscles in his side and had to go to hospital. Peter Eyre pulled a muscle in his groin while Brian Jackson did the same, soon after dismissing Geoffrey Boycott. It left Edwin and Derek Morgan to bowl almost unchanged for the rest of the day. Edwin's final figures were 55-21-117-4 and he also held four catches.

At one point he bowled 37 successive overs and at the tea interval reportedly went straight into the bar for a pint. He laughs at the memory.

> I did, but it was only for a pint of shandy, nothing like the old days when something stronger was how some players got through a long day in the field. I remember being very tired that night though – and no wonder!

Derbyshire finished ninth, exactly mid-table, in 1965. The batting was a major disappointment, Ian Hall heading the averages with 1162 runs at a modest 26, while no one else exceeded 21. Yet for Edwin it was a summer in which he cemented his reputation as one of the best finger spinners in the country.

Once again he conceded only two runs an over, offering his captain control on even the best of wickets. While not running through sides in a summer that was made for seam bowling, he was a priceless asset to a side that struggled to mount a worthwhile total, taking regular and important wickets while conceding very few runs.

Only Brian Jackson bowled more overs than Edwin in 1965 (Rhodes also bowled more overs than Smith, in the Championship). At the end of the summer Edwin returned to Grassmoor, to prepare for his long-awaited testimonial year in 1966. The Smith family expanded once more when a second daughter, Fay, was born on 6 November 1965.

A month previously he sustained a bad injury while working down the mine at Grassmoor, damaging ankle ligaments. This kept him off work

SCORE CARD PRICE 6d.   Toss won by SOUTH AFRICA
This Card does not necessarily include the fall of the last wicket

DERBYSHIRE v SOUTH AFRICANS

Queens Park, Chesterfield June 26th, 28th, 29th, 1965

Hours of Play—   Lunch—1.30 p.m.
First Day 11.30 to 6.30 Second Day 11.30 to 6.30 Third Day 11.30 to 6 or 6.30
Scorers—T G Ryde and M McLennan

DERBYSHIRE	First Innings	Second Innings
1 Eyre J R	run out 36	b Botten 8
2 Hall I W	b Botten 36	lbw b Barlow 23
3 Page M H	b Dumbrill 12	c and b Barlow 27
4 Johnson H L	c Gamsy b Dunbrill 26	not out 44
5 Buxton I R	c Gamsy b Bromfield 0	not out 19
6† Morgan D C	b Macaulay 4	
7 Eyre T J P	c Macaulay b Botten 4	
8 Smith E	c Barlow b Botten 0	
9‡ Taylor R W	not out 14	
10 Rhodes H J	c Barlow b Dumbrill 0	
11 Jackson A B	c Gamsy b Dumbrill 1	

Extras—b-1 lb-7 w- nb-2   10   b- lb-3 w- nb-2 5

Umpires—J S Buller, M.B.E. and J F Crapp

                  Total 143   Total 126

Fall of Wickets—First Innings   Second Innings

1	2	3	4	5	6	7	8	9	10	1	2	3	4	5	6	7	8	9	10
75	83	115	116	122	128	128	128	131	143	20	57	69							

Bowling Analysis—	O	M	R	W	O	M	R	W
Macaulay	17	9	12	1	7	2	14	0
Botten	29	8	55	3	14	2	29	1
Barlow	13	5	23	0	8	4	9	2
Dumbrill	23	11	32	4	10	3	26	0
Bromfield	8	4	11	1	20.3	11	43	0
....	..	..	..	..	..	..	..	..
....	..	..	..	..	..	..	..	..

SOUTH AFRICANS	First Innings	Second Innings
1† P L van Der Merwe	lbw b Rhodes 0	c Taylor b Smith 26
2 E J Barlow	run out 50	c Eyre P b Buxton 23
3‡ D Gamsy	b Rhodes 5	c Buxton b Jackson 10
4 A Bacher	b Rhodes 5	c and b Buxton 5
5 R G Pollock	b Jackson 37	c Hall b Smith 5
6 K C Bland	b Smith 29	c Taylor b Buxton 12
7 D Lindsay	b Jackson 1	b Morgan 13
8 R Dumbrill	c Morgan b Rhodes 7	run out 3
9 J T Botten	lbw b Smith 1	b Jackson 7
10 M J Macaulay	run out 4	b Jackson 7
11 H D Bromfield	not out 0	not out 0

Extras—b-2 lb-3 w-1 nb-3   9   b-4 lb-3 w- nb-1 8

† Captain   ‡ Wicket-keeper

                  Total 149   Total 119

Fall of Wickets—First Innings   Second Innings

1	2	3	4	5	6	7	8	9	10	1	2	3	4	5	6	7	8	9	10
11	25	95	125	130	134	134	141	148	149	21	38	41	64	94	100	100	112	115	119

Bowling Analysis—	O	M	R	W	O	M	R	W
Jackson	19	6	32	2	18	5	35	3
Rhodes	15.3	5	35	4	1	0	3	0
Morgan	6	2	16	0	13	4	19	1
Buxton	6	2	8	0	14	7	16	3
Smith	23	10	43	2	19.4	11	29	2
Eyre P	2	0	6	0	..	..	..	..
Eyre J	..	..	..	..	5	1	9	0

Scorecard for the South Africa match.

for four months but thankfully he was fit for the start of the 1967 cricket season. He was aided in his rehabilitation by Chesterfield Football Club, where he went to run around the pitch as his ankle improved. He was also grateful for the assistance of the club physio, Olly Thomson, who worked on his ankle 'as he would have done for one of his footballers', according to Edwin.

As a consequence, Edwin moved to a new position in the Coal Board offices in Mansfield Woodhouse, a job he held for the next two winters.

Edwin arrives at Scarborough on another occasion,
for a match between Yorkshire and the MCC in 1956.

Chapter Fifteen

Testimonial year

Fifteen years after he made his county debut and 12 years after being awarded his county cap, Edwin finally had his testimonial.

A great deal of work went into the winter months, organising events, cricket matches and personal appearances, There was a testimonial brochure to arrange and articles to commission, while advertisers had to be sourced too. Contact had to be made with many people to get an eleven for a proposed match against a 'Television All-Stars' side, while the star game was scheduled for Sunday 24 July against the ever-popular Rothman's Cavaliers.

Later to become the International Cavaliers, it was an invitation side consisting of current and recently retired international players, with a selection of county cricketers, league professionals and promising youngsters. The mix varied from season to season and match to match, but the games were always entertaining. Before the John Player League captured the public imagination on Sundays, their fixtures proved a big draw around the country, as well as capturing a sizeable audience on BBC2 television between 1965 and 1968.

Sport had previously been seen as an improper use of the medium on the Sabbath, but Huw Wheldon, Controller of Programmes for BBC Television, thought the Cavaliers could fill five hours and gain an audience. He was summoned before the BBC Board of Governors to explain, as he told in his Richard Dimbleby Lecture in 1976.

When he trotted out the names of those likely to be involved, including Ted Dexter, Colin Cowdrey, Garry Sobers, Denis Compton and Godfrey Evans, Wheldon said that the Board reacted 'as if he had named the 12 apostles'. All objections were instantly removed.

The game against them would have been a money-spinner for Edwin, but sadly the match was abandoned without a ball being bowled.

> It was a blow, but thankfully I had the game insured, so still got something out of it. Some of the other games suffered a similar fate, but Leslie Crowther was good enough to bring some of his showbiz friends and there were a few top jockeys involved.

> There was a lot of hard work and there were a few hiccups along the way, but I was grateful for everyone's support and it raised a tidy sum for those days.

The various events raised £2810 for Edwin (about £46,000 in today's value). At the time it was the sixth highest for a Derbyshire player and gave some appreciated financial security to Edwin and his young family.

Over the years there had been many cricketers who struggled to maintain form while managing the demands of their benefit or testimonial, but in 1966, the reverse was true for Edwin. In the words of Derek Morgan in the following season's year book, 'He bowled magnificently and must now be one of the best slow bowlers in the country. Whatever the wicket, he can be relied upon to bowl well.'

By July he was top of the national bowling averages with 40 wickets at eight runs each, just ahead of Derek Underwood. First innings figures of 26-12-26-6 inspired a win against Surrey at The Oval, while his return to the attack, with the home side needing 11 to win with four wickets in hand, saw him take two wickets to inspire a seven-run victory.

Against Hampshire at Chesterfield he returned match figures of 13 for 119, only heavy rain on the last afternoon preventing another win. At Bristol, he took four wickets before lunch, then pulled a muscle in his side that prevented him playing in the next game at Tunbridge Wells, against Kent.

He travelled with the side and was heartened by an exchange between England captain Colin Cowdrey and the Derbyshire physio, Sam Weaver. 'Get him fit, Sam', said Cowdrey, 'We might be needing him for the Test side before long.'

Edwin missed only the one match, but the call never came. Perhaps as well, he says.

> That was a very good West Indian batting side. Sobers was the star, of course, but Conrad Hunte, Basil Butcher, Rohan Kanhai and Seymour Nurse were all fine players. They racked up a lot of runs that summer and it's a pity that it wasn't a weaker touring side, where the selectors may have been more prepared to experiment with players.

Nevertheless his fine form continued. Five for 23 against Warwickshire at Buxton inspired an eight-wicket win, while at Old Trafford, left only 120 to win, Lancashire lost by 30 runs after a 19-over spell from Edwin brought figures of six for 21.

At Trent Bridge, a marathon effort of 41-4-64-4 inspired another eight-wicket victory and in every match he took wickets and bowled accurately in a golden summer.

That made it all the more surprising for him when, at the start of August, he was told that he was left out of the side for the visit of Gloucestershire to the County Ground in Derby. It was a miserable spell of weather, with regular showers and a strong wind, which had caused water to get underneath the covers. It was, in short, a ready-made wicket for a spin bowler in prime form.

> Derek Morgan told me to have a rest and they went with a five-man seam attack, which made no sense. So I packed my bags and went home for a couple of days. As it turned out, Peter Eyre didn't bowl a

ball and they ended up bowling Mike Page's occasional off spin. I could have understood being left out it if I had eight wickets at 40 each, but I had 40-odd at eight each and felt as fit as a fiddle.

There was little play on the first two days but on the last there were three declarations that left us 119 to get in 95 minutes. We didn't last an hour and were bowled out for just 58 by their spinners, who took eight wickets between them.

Edwin was back in the side for the game against Worcestershire at Ilkeston the following day, where his figures of five for 74 and three for 33 should have inspired another win, before the batting collapsed yet again and his side lost by three runs. Then came another five wickets against Worcestershire at Kidderminster, ahead of a trip to Coventry for an eventful game against Warwickshire.

We made 281 in the first innings, largely thanks to Derek's 96, then Brian Jackson found a 'spot' on the wicket and bowled them out for 38. He took eight for 18 and was just about unplayable.

They batted better in the second innings, but Brian, who was a very good bowler, took four more wickets and I bowled a long spell.

That long spell again highlighted his stamina and ability to remain accurate while doing so. The figures are worthy of repetition on a wicket that favoured seam bowlers: 53-25-65-3.

In August, John Arlott wrote an appreciation of Edwin in The Cricketer magazine. In it, he cited the many challenges faced by off spin bowlers over the period of the bowler's career and said:

Edwin has endured primarily because he is a first-class bowler ... Now, at 32, he is a better bowler than he has ever been before: thoughtful, controlled, thrifty and penetrative. He is, too, keen and fit enough to carry on for some years to come.

He ended the summer with 87 Championship wickets at 18, top of the averages for the county. While his batting declined badly and his highest score was only 22, he had bowled more overs than anyone else and had made a major contribution towards an eventual finish in ninth place. Not bad for a side that constantly seemed to struggle for runs.

We had some good batsmen, but they weren't consistent. Laurie Johnson retired at the end of the summer, having averaged less than 20, while Derek Morgan was top and only managed 24 runs per innings. Someone usually got a few runs, but there were rarely enough contributions to set imposing totals.

Teams leaving us small totals to chase always fancied their chances, because once we started losing wickets we seemed to go to pieces.

Mick Allen also left at the end of the summer, being unable to discover the form of his best days. Meanwhile, two young players had joined the staff, both of them set to make a big impression on Edwin and the county cricket scene.

Alan Ward first joined the staff in 1965 and we were very impressed by him. He was quick but raw and took three wickets in the Gillette Cup match against Essex at Chesterfield, when we had a few injuries.

Over the next few seasons, Alan exploded on to the scene, though at that time he was very skinny and obviously needed to work on his strength and fitness. He played two first-class matches in 1966 but broke down and couldn't bowl in the second innings of either.

Fred Swarbrook had looked a very good player for Derbyshire Schools and could score runs and bowl impressive slow left-arm. I was impressed by him and he turned into a very able county cricketer, definitely the best of his kind that I played with at Derbyshire.

It had been a fine season for Edwin, one of his best. When he had some days off he continued, as he had always done, to go back to Grassmoor and work a day or two in the engineer's office, or the fitting shop. It repaid them for letting him off to play cricket throughout the summer and for keeping his job open. He didn't get paid for doing so, but, in the manner of the man, he felt that it was the right thing to do.

The season 1967 was marked by steady improvement. The side moved to sixth in the table and lost only five games all summer, although only the same number were won. As the season progressed, an opening partnership became established that would prove very effective over the following seasons, despite the very different routes into the game for the players concerned. Again, Edwin explains.

David Smith came out of the Yorkshire leagues and was a typically gritty left-hander. He took over the mantle from Ian Hall, who had suffered a serious leg injury and missed many matches. David wasn't often a free-scoring player, but he was very effective for several seasons, as well as proving a very safe slip fielder.

I remember batting well against Glamorgan and making a few runs in the lower order, almost catching up David, who had opened the batting, in the process. Eventually, I played one shot too many and holed out. As I walked past Peter Walker, he said to me 'Can you not take that other fella with you? We're fed up watching him bat'.

Peter Gibbs was different. He had learned his game on good wickets and came to us from Oxford University, where he could play his expansive drives with confidence on that square. He was a lovely, stylish player and was a pleasure to watch when he got going, which was often.

The two players were both impressed by their side's leading spinner. David Smith lived in Chesterfield for some time and got to know Edwin well.

'Tat' and myself travelled together for a number of years and when you share a car with someone for that length of time you get to know them very well. Edwin, although a working class lad, like most of us in those days was blessed with manners better associated with the

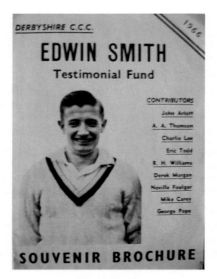

Testimonial brochure.

In the nets, 1966.

Victorian era. He was always smartly dressed, clean shaven and frankly a fine ambassador for his county. I can't recall Edwin having major disagreements with players he played with or against.

Meanwhile, Peter Gibbs remembers him for a different reason.

I'd played in the Varsity Match at Lord's [1966] and found myself on the same ground for Middlesex v Derbyshire and my county debut. I was posted to long on for Edwin and my main memory of the game is running in to take a regulation catch - but on my chest, rather than in my hands.

Despite my state school education, perhaps he thought better of cursing a 'Blue'. In fact he was generously undemonstrative, which almost made my embarrassment worse.

Back at Derby, I thought it politic to ask the 'senior pro' if he had advice on playing there. 'Yes', he said, 'keep your belly to the wind.' Failure to do so meant a stiff back in no time and it was typically sound and succinct advice.

Gibbs just missed a thousand Championship runs in 1967 but Ian Buxton, Derek Morgan and Smith did so and there was a welcome return to his best form from Harold Rhodes, who passed a hundred wickets with ease and led the attack with great skill and impressive pace. Good seam support came from Morgan, Brian Jackson and Peter Eyre, while Edwin simply kept on doing what he had done for years.

There were 81 Championship wickets, costing him 22 runs each while conceding only two runs per over. Only once did he take five in an innings, but he regularly chipped in with two, three or four.

First innings points were won against Glamorgan at Chesterfield, largely thanks to his figures of 28-17-29-4. There were three second innings wickets too, supporting the six of Harold Rhodes as the Welsh side clung on desperately for a draw with nine wickets down. Then came five for 57 as Somerset were beaten at Bath, before a momentous day at Ilkeston, against Cambridge University.

The students included Roger Knight, who later played for Surrey, Gloucestershire and Sussex with distinction, while Derbyshire included the 16-year old Fred Swarbrook. With Morgan, Rhodes and Jackson rested, Edwin took on the captaincy for the first time.

He ended the match a winner, too. He and Swarbrook shared a long spell and six wickets, Edwin bowling 55 overs in the last innings.

It was nice to lead the side out as captain and although it was not against a county side, as senior professional it brought home to me that I had a very good chance of taking on the role on a permanent basis when Derek retired.

Winning did me no harm either ...

Another example of his great control came at Northampton, in a low-scoring game played on a slow pitch. After making only 207, Derbyshire gained a 62-run lead thanks to a spell of three for 25 in 19 overs by Edwin, well supported by Phil Russell with his best figures to date.

David Smith's half-century anchored a poor second innings, but Derbyshire came out on top by just four runs, Edwin's spell of 25-12-36-3 exerting the requisite control when it looked like the home side would win.

There were over 500 runs for Edwin in another excellent summer's work, where the signs were that a new side was coming together. The experience of Rhodes, Morgan Jackson and Smith were helping along less experienced players and there was a degree of optimism come autumn.

Chapter Sixteen

Match-winning captain

Nineteen sixty-eight marked the retirement of Brian Jackson, after six years of service and exemplary bowling. He was underrated, destined to live in the shadow of his namesake, Les, but a very fine bowler, as Edwin explains.

> He had the ability to produce a ball that was unplayable. He called it his 'instant hob-shatterer' and even if a batsman was well set and the wicket doing nothing, Brian could conjure up this special ball that would make those coming next wonder what on earth was happening.

Jackson was no athlete and was a genuine tail-ender with no pretensions to batting. He also admitted to 'vagrancy' in the field, but all was forgiven as he maintained the long tradition of Derbyshire seam bowling. Life was never easy for opposition batsmen when Jackson ran in from the lake end at Chesterfield, lending outstanding support to Harold Rhodes from the pavilion end.

While figures never give the full value of a man, 457 wickets at under 19 confirmed that Brian Jackson was a very good bowler indeed.

Harold Rhodes led the wicket-taking once more, with 99 Championship wickets at 17, but while Peter Eyre lent solid support, the rest of the seam attack suffered injuries, otherwise Derbyshire's final position would have been higher than eighth.

The scoring of points changed, an inducement being made towards more aggressive batting. Sides could now earn one point for every 25 runs they scored over the first 150 in the first 85 overs of their first innings. In the field, there was one point to be earned for every two wickets in those 85 overs. Previously, the battle for first innings ascendancy had produced attritional cricket, with a conclusive result sometimes almost an afterthought. The rationale was that batsmen and bowlers would now be more positive.

Only two sides earned more batting points than Derbyshire in a summer in which the top six batsmen all passed a thousand Championship runs. With Peter Eyre and Edwin each contributing well down the order, the side batted better than for several seasons.

As the lone spinner, Edwin's workload was substantial and he bowled over 900 overs in the County Championship. His 88 wickets represented his second most prolific season and there were seven five-wicket hauls.

The stand out was against Sussex at Chesterfield, where despite Edwin's

An enforced rest day at Bath, 1968. Mike Page, Peter Eyre, David Smith, Edwin Smith, John Harvey, Bob Taylor, Ian Buxton, Peter Gibbs, Brian Jackson.

The batsman, studious in defence.

best efforts the game ended in a draw. Figures of five for 31 and six for 89 did not allow enough time for the runs to be knocked off. Gloucestershire were beaten at Queen's Park, Edwin's six for 57 spinning his side to victory on the final day, but nine wickets against Lancashire at Southport could not prevent a heavy defeat.

It was a summer where overseas players were seen for the first time and some of the best began to appear around the counties. The greatest of them all, Garfield Sobers, turned out for neighbouring Nottinghamshire, while Majid Jahangir, later to be known as Majid Khan, enhanced Glamorgan. Fellow Pakistan international Mushtaq Mohammad played for Northamptonshire, while Rohan Kanhai gave excellent service to Warwickshire. Meanwhile, two young South Africans, Mike Procter and Barry Richards, gave a hint of things to come for Gloucestershire and Hampshire respectively, the former taking six wickets against Derbyshire at Chesterfield, despite a fine century from Mike Page. He had at last married talent to weight of runs, as Edwin explains.

> Mike had looked a good player when he first got into the team, but like Laurie Johnson it took him a while to realise his talent. After that, the runs started to flow and he was a lovely player to watch, his best shots all in front of the wicket.

> In addition, Mike had a terrific pair of hands and held some blinding catches. He was especially good at short leg, but anywhere close he ranked among the best in the country.

A young, highly-rated Australian played the season for Somerset, but was frustrated when the game between the two sides at Bath was rained off without a ball being bowled. So violent were the storms at the end of the first day that several bridges were washed away in the Pen valley. With the ground under four to five feet of water in places and deckchairs bobbing across the outfield, the game was abandoned at the end of the second day.

In the return at Buxton, Greg Chappell, soon to become one of the world's finest batsmen, was dismissed twice by Derbyshire's wily off spinner, as Derbyshire won a tight match by two wickets. For once, Edwin had forgotten about something.

> Did I really get him twice? You know, I'd forgotten all about that. I suppose he was just a young player at the time, learning the game and I thought little of it. Mind you, it's not a bad thing to have on the CV, is it?

The highlight of the summer was the match against the visiting Australians at Chesterfield. Batting first, they made 259, largely thanks to a typically aggressive 95 from Doug Walters. Derek Morgan took five for 83, while Edwin had four for 80.

In reply, Derbyshire slipped to 79 for five, before Bob Taylor and Derek Morgan joined forces to avoid the follow-on. Coming in just before the close, Edwin hit three boundaries in the day's final over, then next morning launched an assault on off spinner Ashley Mallett, who was hit for 14 from one over. Edwin reached a fine 50 with a six and seven fours before holing out, a lead of 74 being conceded.

Openers John Inverarity and Ian Redpath both made sixties before Edwin dismissed them both, but Brian Jackson took four wickets and the tourists collapsed from 234 for three to 270 all out, leaving Derbyshire 345 to win.

They had reached 91 for two by the close, with Peter Gibbs going well, but he went early the next morning and at 97 for four, the game looked over. John Harvey had other ideas and added 74 with Derek Morgan, then an unbroken 39 with Peter Eyre by lunch, which was taken with the score 210 for five.

The partnership continued after lunch and the score reached 261 before Eyre was caught down the leg side. Bob Taylor helped to add 30, but then he and Harvey were out quickly, the latter for a fine 92. Edwin and Harold Rhodes added 28, seam bowler David Renneberg being hit for ten in an over, before Rhodes played on to Neil Hawke.

With 26 required, Edwin farmed the bowling and scored 12 runs in the next two overs, before Renneberg returned for one last spell. Edwin cut his first ball for four, before edging a fast leg cutter into the safe hands of Ian Chappell at slip. He was out for 31 and Derbyshire lost by nine runs, on a pitch that the visitors thought the best they had played on during the tour.

It was a wonderful advert for cricket and Edwin's fine summer was capped by being made captain for six matches, taking over from Derek Morgan after the first innings against Worcestershire at Kidderminster, when the latter pulled a hamstring while batting.

Still showing a penchant for Worcestershire's batting after all the years, figures of 29.3-17-37-5 in the first innings established a stranglehold on the game that Harold Rhodes ensured was not released in the second. A feature of his captaincy was his willingness to bowl the young Fred Swarbrook, who took two wickets in each innings while adhering to the accepted economy rate that Edwin had set over the years. It spoke well of the 17-year old, but equally so of a captain who had faith in him.

> Fred was a lovely lad. He stayed with his grandparents around the corner from the County Ground, so he was handy for the training sessions. He was a player who responded to an arm around the shoulder and gentle encouragement, but tended to sulk and withdraw into himself if someone had a go at him.

> He developed into a really good county cricketer. He was never an athlete, but he had a good pair of hands, became a very handy batsman and was a wicket-taking bowler. There was a lot to like in Fred.

Edwin skippered the side in six other Championship matches that summer, as Morgan later sustained a dislocated finger against Middlesex at Lord's. One of those matches, the return against Worcestershire, was won, another two were rain-ruined, two were drawn and only one lost. That was against Nottinghamshire at Ilkeston, where Garfield Sobers proved to be the difference between the two sides, playing a brilliant innings on an awkward wicket.

Mike Page was impressed by Edwin's captaincy in those matches.

> Edwin was quiet, undemonstrative. He knew the game inside out and, as you would expect from such an experienced bowler, set some canny fields. He didn't over-bowl himself either, which is sometimes a temptation and I know that most of the players were quietly impressed by the way that he went about things.

As the summer drew to a close, Alan Ward became established in the first team, replacing Brian Jackson as the opening partner for Harold Rhodes. He made a huge early impression, according to Edwin.

> He was like a firework exploding onto the county scene. In the last three matches he took 23 wickets and there were a few batsmen who didn't fancy him at all. You must understand that at the end of the season, people were starting to think of what they would be doing through the winter. Then this lad appears and is as fast as anyone on the circuit, probably faster.

> He took ten wickets in the match at Cardiff, where it was lifting sharply at one end. Nobody played him with confidence and we were glad he was on our side. At that stage, he looked like an outstanding prospect.

Chapter Seventeen
Lord's in the summer of '69

For Derbyshire fans of a certain vintage, 1969 was a season in which the side suggested, for the first time, that they could play one day cricket. That argument was not substantiated in the first season of the John Player County League, where only five matches were won all summer and the side finished third bottom, but a Gillette Cup run finished in the most memorable of semi-finals and the excitement, but ultimate frustration, of a Lord's final.

The Sunday competition was enjoyed by spectators, though less so by the players. Sundays had been rest days, with only an occasional charity or benefit match to disturb the tranquillity and opportunity for a game of golf. Now they had to change grounds, more often than not, to play a one-day game in the middle of a County Championship match. Little wonder that some players and teams failed to cope.

At least, for Derbyshire, the switch of grounds was usually local. The vast expanse of The Oval was replaced by the more intimate, tree-lined Sutton for the season opener and home games saw a drive to Chesterfield, Derby, Buxton, Burton-on-Trent or Ilkeston from the previous day's venue.

Thankfully the roads had improved dramatically and there was nowhere near the traffic of later years. It all made for a demanding season for players, but not especially so for Edwin Smith.

When he stepped out for the county in their third last Sunday game of the summer, it was his first one-day appearance for over four years. It was also, on 24 August, the first time in 1969 that Derbyshire had fielded anything other than a full seam attack in one-day cricket. The irony was not lost on Edwin that, in a narrow defeat to Leicestershire, he still didn't bowl. He did make second top score, a breezy unbeaten 21, but it was not enough to save a side that had become bogged down while chasing only a modest total.

His only other appearance was in the summer's last John Player County League fixture, against Hampshire at Bournemouth. He was only selected as Mike Page and Harold Rhodes had sustained injuries in the previous day's Lord's final, while Ian Buxton had been released to his football duties. Edwin bowled just five overs for 23 runs, although was only introduced as the sixth bowler, while Fred Swarbrook, also making his season one-day debut, didn't bowl at all.

All very strange. Lancashire won the first Sunday title, narrowly pipping Hampshire, who in turn edged out Essex. The red rose county's success

Edwin's Gillette Cup medal.

Derek Morgan holds a typically sharp catch from Edwin's bowling,
George Emmett of Gloucestershire the victim.
George Dawkes behind the stumps.

was built around keen fielding, aggressive batting and a varied attack, including left-arm spinner David Hughes and off spinner Jack Simmons. Peter Sainsbury - flat, slow left-arm for Hampshire - and another left-armer, Ray East, with Yorkshire's Don Wilson, were three of the seven most prolific wicket-takers, suggesting that spin could not only survive in the format, but flourish. It does pose the question as to why Derbyshire were so staid in their approach.

Perhaps the answer came in the new recruit for the summer. Fred Rumsey had given long and distinguished service to Somerset, after starting his career at Worcestershire. He had played five Test matches for England and had founded the Professional Cricketers Association in 1967. This gave players a greater say in the administration of the game and saw standard contracts and a minimum wage for the first time.

Rumsey had taken up a position as Public Relations Officer for the club, who registered him to play in one-day cricket. He could still bowl tight lines and gave little away, although his fielding was mediocre at best and he had few pretensions as a batsman. He became a key member of the Derbyshire attack, alongside Harold Rhodes and Alan Ward. With Ian Buxton and Derek Morgan to offer all-round skills alongside Peter Eyre, it meant that Derbyshire's bowling largely selected itself, even if it left a worryingly long tail.

As it transpired, the march to Lord's was played on wickets that helped those seam bowlers. Somerset were beaten at Taunton by three wickets, where Rumsey took three for 19 against his old employers, who made only 144. Then Worcestershire were beaten by four wickets, the winning target this time only 157.

The third round took Derbyshire to Cardiff and on a damp pitch Rhodes' four for 17 was decisive in bowling Glamorgan out for 117. Taking few risks, the county eased to a win by nine wickets, setting up a home tie against Sussex. While not quite the one-day force they had been, they were losing finalists in 1968 and had beaten Derbyshire by ten wickets at Hove on the way to that final. They batted long and usually opted for an all-seam attack themselves, in which future England captain Tony Greig and fast bowler John Snow played key parts.

A crowd of 10,582 was recorded as being present for the semi-final, though how much of the action was seen by some is a moot point. The ground was still wet from heavy rain earlier in the week, but groundsman Harold Graham and his team ensured a prompt start was possible. Some of the rain had got under the covers so Derek Morgan opted to bat first on a wet pitch, mindful of how it may cut up later.

The home side mustered only 136. Few among the huge crowd gave Derbyshire a chance, but in a tense atmosphere Alan Ward began in complete silence from the pavilion end. After a no-ball, Ward forced Les Lenham to play on with his fourth delivery. Four maiden overs followed, before Ken Suttle edged Harold Rhodes for four – remarkably, the only scoring shot off the veteran bowler in seven overs.

Ward bowled Graham Cooper and after 14 overs; Sussex were only 10 for two. Nor did the change bowlers allow respite, Rumsey's nine overs conceding only 13 runs for two wickets, while at the other end, Peter Eyre had the greatest day of his career. Edwin takes up the story.

> Peter was an unlucky player with injury and illness over the years, but on that day he could do no wrong. He perhaps benefited from the efforts of Harold, Alan and Fred, taking wickets as Sussex perhaps saw him as the 'weak link' that they had to attack. He wasn't though, he was a very good, fully committed bowler who hit the right line and length on a regular basis. Certainly he did that day!

Eyre finished with the remarkable figures of 10.2-4-18-6 as Sussex slumped to 49 all out. It had taken them 35 overs of batting against a disciplined seam attack in the finest Derbyshire tradition.

Many people expected the county's opponents to be the Sobers-inspired Nottinghamshire, but Yorkshire beat them with some ease at Scarborough to set up a northern showdown at Lord's on 6 September.

In the intervening month, Derbyshire won only one of their five Sunday matches and played some dismal cricket. They were twice dismissed for under 100 and once only just managed to scrape past it. The batting was lamentably brittle, and the portents for the Gillette Cup final were not good.

It was the same story in the County Championship. Only three matches were won all summer, as the side finished second bottom. Only Mike Page and Peter Gibbs passed the thousand-run benchmark and the rest struggled for form.

Of the attack, only Harold Rhodes and Alan Ward passed 50 wickets among the seam bowlers, the former at 33, not bowling the same pace as before and perhaps feeling the effects of a pre-season crash on an icy German autobahn. Ward finished top of the averages with 57 wickets at 13, but missed a number of games through injury. Who was the quickest, at his peak? Edwin is well-placed to answer.

> Harold, definitely. Alan was quick and in the late 1960s and very early 1970s was perhaps as quick as anyone in the game. He was very selective as to when he put in the hard yards though, and his fitness was a worry from the start. If the wicket was in his favour, Alan would bend his back; if it wasn't, he didn't often try to make things happen.

> Harold did. In the late 1950s through to the mid-1960s you wouldn't have swapped him for anyone in the country. He was fast *and* accurate, things that don't always go together and even on a good wicket he would bowl some really quick balls that brought results.

> He paced himself, like the best fast bowlers learn to do, but Harold was a very fine bowler. At times, when I fielded at short leg for him, I used to whistle as one flew past the batsman. A few of them did too!

Edwin took 51 wickets in the County Championship, but often got on as only fourth or fifth change, as the county fixation with seam continued. Seven seam bowlers appeared during the summer, one of them a young lad from Darley Dale named Mike Hendrick, who made an early impression.

Mike bowled accurately and moved the ball around, but at that stage he looked like a good feed would do him good! He needed time to fill out and when he did, he became an international bowler, as we all know.

He was a nice lad and eager to learn. Like all the best Derbyshire bowlers, he didn't like giving away easy runs and so bowled just short of a length. Sometimes he got criticism for that, but he became a very fine bowler.

By the time the Lord's final arrived, Edwin had been bowling well and with the usual accuracy. His four for 43 had contributed to a win over Lancashire at Blackpool, while match figures of four for 82 in 35 overs could not prevent a loss to Northamptonshire. Edwin travelled to Lord's with the Derbyshire squad and takes up the story.

I was bowling well. A month earlier, I had taken five for 73 in an innings against Yorkshire at Chesterfield. I usually did well against them and that day I bowled 39 overs and only had a three-over break! So I was hopeful I might get picked for the final. Besides my record against Yorkshire, Lord's was a ground where spinners normally did well. Certainly Fred Titmus got his share of wickets there over the years!

The night before the game, we had a team meeting in the hotel and there was no indication of the final eleven. We chatted about the game as a team and agreed that if Derek won the toss, we should bat and set them a total to chase.

The next day, he went out to toss and came back in to the pavilion shortly afterwards.

'We've won the toss and we're bowling,' he said. 'Edwin, you're not playing, Fred – you're in.'

I was stunned. A few players were, as Derek had changed his mind and completely ignored what we had discussed the previous evening. We bowled six seam bowlers that day and Yorkshire got too many because of the lack of variety. It had served us well in previous rounds, but Lord's was a different wicket and needed different tactics.

Would it have changed the result if I had played? Maybe not, but they'd have had to think a bit more about how to get their runs and I don't think they would have got as many.

Spinner Don Wilson took three wickets for Yorkshire in the final, Yorkshire's 219 for eight always looking beyond an insipid batting line-up that was weakened further when Mike Page injured his side in catching Brian Close. Edwin came on as twelfth man to replace him, but could only look on as Yorkshire passed 200, a challenging score at that time in the one-day game.

After a steady but slow opening stand between Gibbs and Smith, the Derbyshire innings fell quickly behind the required rate and there was a hint of desperation in the elevation of Alan Ward to number four in the order. There were a few bucolic blows from Ian Buxton, but Derbyshire subsided to 150 all out and were well beaten.

It was a disappointing end to the season and was to get worse for Edwin, as long time team mates Derek Morgan and Harold Rhodes announced their retirement. At 40, Morgan was understandably not the player he once was, but the retirement of Rhodes, at 33, was a shock. Edwin explains:

> Derek had a huge workload over many years and it was only in his last year that the standards slipped. He started to pick up injuries and it became harder to play through them. He must have been one of the best players who never represented his country and the presence of Trevor Bailey kept a very good player from a wider audience.

> He wasn't as good a captain as Guy Willatt or Donald Carr and tended to be reactive, rather than proactive. Games were allowed to drift and I had the impression that spin was something of an afterthought for Derek, once all seam bowling options had been explored.

> Harold had business opportunities and opted to take them, telling Derbyshire that he would be available for one-day matches in the same way that Fred Rumsey was. Nothing was done about it, until Nottinghamshire approached him and sought permission for his services. They offered him a game every week, we didn't, so Harold took their offer with some regret.

> It was poorly handled and a disappointing way to treat one of the best players the county ever had.

Harold confirms the story:

> I had taken up a post as a brewery representative, but had been approached by Reg Simpson at Nottinghamshire to see if I would be interested in playing some one-day cricket for them. I rang up Eddie Gothard, the Derbyshire treasurer at the time and said that I would prefer to offer my services to the club I had played for, if they wanted to retain my registration.

> He said no, adding that they were only interested in players who could play all the time. I couldn't understand it, because I was playing with Burnley in the Lancashire League and keeping fit, not just wandering in off the street. Fred Rumsey was not contracted full-time, but they played him without question. So I went and played for Nottinghamshire, where I changed next to Garfield Sobers!

With Morgan retired, Derbyshire needed a new captain and for many people Edwin Smith was the right man. The Derby Evening Telegraph had run a piece as early as 1968, suggesting that Edwin was the man to take over when Derek Morgan retired. It was based on precedent, as Harold Rhodes explains:

Edwin was the senior professional and had been on the staff since 1951. Since the end of the amateur-professional divide, the Derbyshire 'way', as with other counties, was to give the captaincy to the senior man on the staff.

Instead, Ian Buxton was offered and accepted the captaincy. Ian was a good man and a decent cricketer, but in my opinion, Edwin should have been the next captain. I actually went to the club committee, without his knowledge, to state Edwin's case, but to no avail.

Buxton had captained the side in two drawn matches against Oxford University and Somerset in June, but Edwin had led the side against Northamptonshire in September, adding to his experience from the previous year. As an all-rounder, Buxton was a key member of the side in all forms of the game. Edwin, through no fault of his own, was not, but he knew the game inside out, as Mike Page explains:

Edwin was very shrewd tactically. I had a lot of time for him, but I think the deciding thing for the committee at that time was the respective backgrounds of the players.

Ian was grammar school educated and a better 'fit' for the role, whereas Edwin came from a mining background. Like it or not, we weren't too far from when captains were gentleman amateurs and the role carried certain responsibilities off the field. Don't forget that Ian had a certain stature as a footballer too and that is what the committee went for, in my opinion.

Phil Russell tells a slightly different story.

I don't think Edwin was ever in the running for the captaincy on a permanent basis, simply because he didn't play in the one day games. One-day cricket was becoming more important with the start of the John Player League and generally Edwin wasn't considered for those matches, for whatever reason.

I seem to remember that mid way-through the 1969 season we knew that Ian would be captain the following year.

Fred Swarbrook felt that Edwin was the wrong man for the job for another reason.

Edwin was simply too nice a person to be the team captain. That's not at all a bad thing, but sometimes as the leader you have treat your players a little more harshly and Edwin wasn't that sort of person. In all the time that I knew him, he remained a genuinely lovely man.

It had been a chastening experience for Edwin, but he got his head down and prepared for the 1970 season. It was the club's centenary and marked his 20th summer as a professional cricketer.

Chapter Eighteen
Centenary summer

Quick lessons had been learned after the Lord's final and for 1970 Derbyshire engaged a relatively unknown South African named Chris Wilkins as their first overseas professional. He had impressed in domestic cricket, where one judge had deemed him to have greater potential than Graeme Pollock and Barry Richards. It sounded impressive and there was hope that if he proved successful it would give the side a lift.

Wilkins opened the batting back home but, like many others, before and since, found English early season wickets a challenge. When he moved down the order to number four, it was a different story, as Edwin explains:

> Chris was perhaps the hardest hitter of a cricket ball I have seen. Clive Lloyd was in the same bracket, but Chris simply smashed it. When he was in the mood, the sun was shining and there was a crowd, he was a terrific entertainer, but he paid no attention to the state of the game. He just played the way he wanted to play.

> When it came off it was fantastic. Other times he would frustrate us, because we'd be fighting to avoid defeat and he would try to hit over the top and be caught. In the indoor nets at Derby you could never turn your back on him, because if a bowler over-pitched, he would hit it back like a rocket and we would all be diving for cover!

Wilkins proved a decent signing, with a good pair of hands and an ability to keep wicket in emergencies, as well as being a change bowler with a knack of taking big wickets, dismissing Geoff Boycott on 99 at Chesterfield in 1970 with the assistance of a diving catch from Edwin. He had an extraordinary eye, as former Derbyshire opening batsman, Alan Hill, explains.

> He was the first player I ever saw play what is now called a switch hit. It was in the nets at Derby and he was facing David Wilde, who was a pretty lively left-armer. Chris switched his stance and hands as David was about to let go and absolutely smacked it. We all looked at one another, seriously impressed by the hand-eye coordination.

His signing galvanised the batting, at least for one season. Whatever the private misgivings of some players over the captaincy, Derbyshire's centenary summer was a good one. In the County Championship they finished seventh equal, having been top in early August, but Ian Buxton was later to comment that the position was false, three of the side's seven wins having been achieved with only minutes to spare. Had those matches been drawn, the county would have finished second bottom, the need to strengthen the side then being more apparent.

Three defeats in the last five matches saw the side drop from the lofty heights, but the opening pair of Gibbs and Smith, followed by the aggressive Page and Wilkins was a great success. All passed the thousand run mark with ease, but if they failed it exposed a soft underbelly to the batting that was worrying, despite the best efforts of John Harvey and the new captain.

There was an unfamiliar look to the bowling, at least in three-day cricket. With Rhodes gone and Peter Eyre struggling with glandular fever, it placed a large burden on the shoulders of Alan Ward, who often opened the bowling with Buxton in the absence of alternatives. Phil Russell passed 50 wickets for the first time and made good progress, after slowing down to bowl off cutters. It made for a less intimidating pace attack than previous years, especially when Ward injured an ankle playing for England against the Rest of the World and was seldom fully fit afterwards. His mounting injuries were a concern for the county, as Edwin explains:

> If the recognised ideal build for a fast bowler was short and sturdy with a big backside, like Harold Larwood and Fred Trueman, Alan was the opposite. He had a very long back and the pronounced arch of this, as he let the ball go, put a strain on it, as well as his hamstrings.

> We had to nurse him through matches, giving him very short bursts, but he was less prepared to play through niggles than Cliff, Les, Harold or Brian had been.

It placed an additional burden on the side's veteran off spinner, who bowled nearly 200 overs more than anyone else, taking 73 wickets at a cost of 30. The wickets were better and the influx of overseas stars, with the bonus point system, meant that batsmen were willing to take greater risks. Nevertheless, Edwin still only conceded an admirable two and a half runs an over and remained a focal point of the attack.

For the first time, in Fred Swarbrook, he had a genuine spin bowling foil, the 19-year-old taking 57 Championship wickets and five in an innings on three occasions. Edwin enjoyed bowling with him.

> Fred was a talent. He could bat, too and made a very good 90 as an emergency opener against Essex. At that stage, I looked forward to spending several years working with him while he learned his craft. I was 38, but felt fit and was bowling as well as ever.

The attempt to emulate the previous year's Gillette Cup run ended at Lord's, but this time in the second round against Middlesex, after a first round bye. A total of 161 for nine didn't look enough for Derbyshire and their hosts scrambled to a two-wicket win. Edwin's spell of almost ten overs went for only 35 runs, but he was to play only two more one-day matches that summer.

The first came the following day, in front of the television cameras at Northampton. Derbyshire were top of the John Player League table after four straight wins and initially appeared to have done well, limiting Northamptonshire to 151 all out in their 40 overs. Once again, Edwin wasn't asked to bowl, a decision that seemed all the more strange when Denis Breakwell, the home side's left-arm spinner, bowled eight straight overs and took four wickets for ten.

The other was on 5 July, when a Derbyshire side played the MCC at Chesterfield, in a match played under John Player League rules to mark the club's centenary. The MCC was effectively a Derbyshire old boys side, bolstered by Yorkshire's Phil Sharpe (later to play for the county) and Doug Padgett.

Aged 49, Les Jackson conceded only 34 runs in his eight overs, while at 53, Cliff Gladwin conceded only 19. With 'youngster' Brian Jackson (37) also conceding only 34 runs, the old guard did well, Ian Hall's 81 ensuring that the current side made a competitive 186 for six.

Guy Willatt top scored with 26, exactly half of his age, as the MCC were bowled for 128, with Edwin claiming the wickets of his two captains from the 1950s (Donald Carr the other), as well as Padgett for just 24 runs.

That was his final one-day action of the summer, one in which his side played some very good 40-over cricket, winning 11 of their 16 games and finishing in third. One of the best displays was at Ilkeston, when David Smith's 85 from just 61 balls saw a potentially awkward run chase accomplished with over ten overs to spare. This came just a week after Alan Ward's sensational four wickets in four balls saw another fine win over Sussex, at Derby.

Twice they capitulated badly in front of the television cameras, while second-placed Kent beat them at Maidstone in front of a crowd of 10,000. Derbyshire failed to cope with Derek Underwood, on another wicket where a spinner might have proved useful.

The big game was at Buxton, where eventual champions Lancashire, having been put into bat with rain threatening, amassed 229 for nine on a wicket that helped the bowlers. With the exception of Phil Russell, whose eight overs were remarkably parsimonious and went for only 20 runs, the rest of the attack was put to the sword, after Faroukh Engineer led off with 46 from just 28 deliveries.

Derbyshire never got close and were all out for 115, yet another spinner, David Hughes, taking four wickets. An enormous straight six by Wilkins, still on its way up as it left the ground, was the only highlight for the home side, who were heavily beaten in front of a very vocal crowd, estimated at 8,000.

It was a summer of exciting cricket, marking a new decade and a new century for the club. It was one that suggested a bright future, but it fell apart with undue haste, as Edwin explains.

David Smith retired at the end of the summer to start a career outside the game. Ian Hall had a good summer in 1971 in his place, but then

Edwin's John Player League medal.

*Derbyshire side line up behind a floral display at Queen's Park
in their centenary year: Fred Swarbrook, Peter Gibbs, Alan Ward,
Mike Hendrick, Edwin Smith, Ian Buxton (captain),
John Harvey, Chris Wilkins, Bob Taylor, David Smith, Ian Hall.*

Peter Gibbs retired to concentrate on his writing in 1972 and Ian Buxton retired too. It left us very short of experience and it was the same with the bowling.

Alan's struggles with his fitness reduced his effectiveness for us, although he continued to bowl some very good spells. Peter Eyre had health and injury issues and without them there was a young and not especially hostile attack. Phil Russell was a good bowler and later became an even better coach, but Ian Buxton's effectiveness as a bowler had gone and younger players needed time.

There was hope that, given time, Mike Hendrick might develop into something special, but David Wilde, a left-arm bowler of some pace, drifted quickly out of the game because of concerns over his action.

It left a lot, perhaps too much, on the shoulders of Fred Swarbrook and in what became a vicious circle, the batting struggled at times through the weight of expectation, the need to score enough runs to offset a weakened attack. John Harvey had a solid summer down the order, but Mike Page came back too soon from a winter achilles tendon injury and was far from his best.

Only one County Championship match was won all summer and although only four were lost, there was a perception that too many games began with a draw the summit of ambition. In some ways, given the limitations of the staff, that was understandable, but a few players felt that a willingness to take risks may, at times, have brought dividends.

Some felt that may have happened under Edwin Smith, but he spent what was to be his final season as a cricketer in 1971 as a somewhat peripheral figure in the squad. He played one last Sunday game, against Yorkshire at Harrogate and finished on the winning side, once again not being asked to bowl.

Even at this distance, the failure to utilise an experienced bowler when the side was short of them seems strange and Edwin tells a story of the game against Worcestershire, at Queen's Park.

> Worcestershire lost early wickets, but were recovering thanks to Ted Hemsley and Jim Yardley. Ian Buxton had used five bowlers but I was still kicking my heels in the outfield.

> Then I heard a familiar voice, in a broad Yorkshire accent shout "'ey oop Edwin ... hast tha broke tha arm?" It was Arnold Hamer, walking around the boundary and he said it in a voice that must have been heard by everyone. Inside a couple of overs I was on, had Jim stumped by Bob Taylor and caught and bowled Ted.

In his final season, Edwin took 31 wickets in 13 matches, Swarbrook being preferred as the main spinner. His last five-wicket haul came at Northampton, a final analysis of 28.4-10-65-5 reminiscent of his great days. His final spell came a fortnight later, at The Oval, when he bowled a single atypical over for 13 runs, as Surrey hit out ahead of a declaration. It was a game that his county lost and was typical of a season of disappointment.

Despite this, he had every intention of carrying on, perhaps forcing his way back into the side to bowl alongside Swarbrook, but behind the scenes, things started to move fast. Denis Smith, coach since the retirement of Harry Elliott in 1952, was 65 in January 1972 and announced his retirement. Having moved to the role from senior professional on the field, there was a precedent for a similar move again.

Was Edwin Smith, at 38, ready to become county coach?

> The post was offered to me and after a little thought, I accepted. The previous season had suggested, rightly or wrongly, that I was gradually being eased aside and I had spent a lot of time in the summer working with the National Coal Board.

> I'd had my advanced coaching badge for years and another factor was the potential in two young off spin bowlers, Bob Swindell and Geoff Miller. If I played on, their opportunities would have been limited, although when I started Geoff was still a schoolboy with time on his side.

> You have to go some time, so I announced my retirement and took on the position of county coach.

Chapter Nineteen

An impossible task

It would be wrong to say that Edwin took over as Derbyshire coach when the club was at its lowest ebb. After all, the side of 1920 had lost all but one of its 18 matches, the other rained off without a ball bowled. Yet there was little to shout about for the Derbyshire faithful during another dark period in the club's history. Having finished bottom of the table in 1971 and 1972, they were again in 1974 and only avoided last place by one point in 1973.

The side was not without talent. Mike Page remained a vastly underrated batsman and Bob Taylor was almost without peer as a wicket-keeper, maintaining standards of excellence that would have been impressive in a good side, even more meritorious in one struggling like Derbyshire.

Taylor's undemonstrative glove work earned wickets that at times were not deserved, made the awkward look routine and made the fielding side look better than at times they were. His batting developed only into that of a useful tail-ender, meaning that the better-equipped Alan Knott at Kent kept him from the England side, but most good judges gave the Derbyshire man the edge behind the stumps.

Yet the rest of the side was woefully inexperienced and 1972, Edwin's first as coach, saw Derbyshire win only one Championship match. Alan Ward and Peter Eyre bowled only 260 overs between them and the latter retired at the end of the season. John Harvey, a solid middle order batsman since 1963, had a bad one at the wrong time and was released, while Ian Buxton decided he could do no more and resigned his post in early August. Ian Hall also retired and, with the loss of Peter Gibbs, the club was in crisis.

For Edwin, the writing was on the wall from an early stage.

> When I took over as coach, the first job had to be to get the indoor school into some sort of shape. There was no real heating, only a wood burning stove in the corner, while the floor was covered in bird droppings. My wife and I spent hours scrubbing the floor and then I replaced all the windows myself and got the money back from the club. Major Carr, the club secretary, gave me a tenner for doing the work myself and saving them a bob or two.

> With the place being so cold, the moisture used to seep up through the floor and there were times when we had to put down sawdust, so bowlers and batsmen didn't slip. One night I had to cancel the practice, as it was so wet and Major Carr was concerned we could have a serious injury.

The players would come in for pre-season nets after the New Year, maybe for a couple of hours on either a Saturday or Sunday morning. We had a 'Pitchmastic' artificial wicket in there, a rubberised surface, but when we got the stove going and people sweating, it used to melt! I had to get it taken out, levelled up and green matting put down.

The players changed in the old jockey quarters, the very basic changing rooms of the time, then walked across to the indoor school. It wasn't at all sophisticated and remember – this was in the 1970s!

There were a few decent performances in one-day cricket and batsmen such as Ashley Harvey-Walker, Alan Hill and Tony Borrington suggested potential, as did Harry Cartwright. Later in the decade, all would play key roles in the resurgence of the county under the ebullient South African, Eddie Barlow, but all were then at a formative stage of their careers.

I inherited a staff of 15 players, all of them born in Derbyshire. They needed work and encouragement, but most of all they needed time to develop. Some of them became very good cricketers once they had come to terms with the demands of the game, but you can't fast-track that sort of thing.

It is important to understand how the role of coach worked at the county. Edwin's remit was exactly the same as Denis Smith's before him – to identify and nurture young talent, getting players to a standard where they were good enough for the first team. Senior players rarely crossed his path, unless they were having a poor run of form and wanted some advice. Edwin spent much of his summer coaching young players, captaining the second team and batting at eleven.

The side did well, reaching the semi-final of the Under-25 County Cricket Competition. They progressed through their group unbeaten, winning four matches and seeing two rained off, which saw them drawn against Middlesex in the semi-final at Edgbaston.

Derbyshire struggled to 133 all out in their 20 overs, with Alan Hill, Tony Borrington and Bob Swindell making twenties, but no one going on to a match-defining score. Middlesex had problems in turn and only won by two wickets, largely thanks to 60 from Tim Selwood, no one else making more than 14.

They were impressive sides. Besides those named above, Derbyshire included Mike Hendrick, Fred Swarbrook and Harry Cartwright, who would go on to fine first-class careers. Middlesex, who went on to win the competition by beating Glamorgan in the final, were even stronger. Their side featured future England players John Emburey, Phil Edmonds, Graham Barlow and Mike Selvey, as well as 'Larry' Gomes, who would go on to 60 Test matches for the West Indies.

Edwin was proud of his young charges.

They did very well. We played as a team and bowled tight, while fielding well throughout the competition. Sadly we conceded 24 extras in that semi-final, which probably cost us the game. There were lads in the side who went on to good cricket careers, but two who played that summer felt their futures better served outside of the game.

Godfrey Smith was a lovely, stylish batsman who never made the final step to the first team for some reason. He was a good player to watch and it was a shame he was perhaps just short of the county game standard.

Chris Armishaw had some senior one-day games and looked a good bowler with definite long-term potential. He took four wickets in one match, but he had a good career in banking, which he felt was a better long-term option.

The first team attack was well led in all forms of the game by the fast-improving Mike Hendrick and reinforcements arrived for John Player League matches in the shape of Yorkshire legend Fred Trueman. His signing was an attempt to boost attendances, but at the age of 41 his best days were well behind him. The action was still majestic, but he had been retired for three seasons and it showed both in the field and in the final product.

The signing was a strange one. Was Edwin involved?

No. Any signings were made on the recommendation of the captain and with the authority of the committee. Sometimes the latter may have felt that a particular signing had merit and would just do it. Some of them were hard for me to understand, if I am honest, but it wasn't my area. Rightly or wrongly, I kept my head down and did what I was paid to do.

Various names were mentioned as potential Derbyshire players, including Tom Graveney and Peter Parfitt. Newspapers suggested that Australian fast bowler Dennis Lillee would be the club's new overseas signing, a move eventually scuppered by a serious back injury.

The need for overseas recruitment came about when Chris Wilkins decided that he wanted to stay in South Africa at the end of the 1972 season, after three summers with the club. A new overseas player topped the shopping list and it was here, for the only time, that the committee acted upon a recommendation from the coach.

Indian Test off spinner Srinivasan Venkataraghavan, more commonly known as Venkat, was a bowler of high quality, who fielded well close to the wicket, and was a handy batsman. The rationale was that such a bowler might help to bring on Geoff Miller and Bob Swindell, two off spinners of potential, while lending support to Fred Swarbrook when he returned to the staff. It was a move that ignored what appeared to be a greater need for a reliable batsman, while the encouragement of the young players didn't go as planned, as Edwin explains:

As the senior spinner, Venkat got choice of ends, which should have been the case. Because Geoff was a good batsman, we ended up playing two off spinners, with Fred Swarbrook bowling at what was seen as the least responsive end. Geoff got on after Venkat, but Bob Swindell lacked opportunity and drifted out of the first-class game.

The signing didn't work as I expected and I admit that. He took wickets but often at a cost that we could ill-afford. Had I played on, I would probably have got those wickets and it would have saved the club a fair bit of money. He certainly got paid more than I did!

Swindell was unlucky. In 1972 he had taken 26 wickets at 31 runs each, getting good turn and bowling with a nice loop, but the following year bowled only 173 overs and finished in 1974, when he played only one match. He is philosophical about his county career.

I had opportunities after Venkat's arrival but failed to take advantage. I had my moments, but was simply too inconsistent to become an established county player. Geoff was developing fast as an all-rounder and with the financial state of the club, I quickly realised there would be no place for three off spinners on the staff.

In many ways it did me a favour to be released in my mid-twenties, as I still had time to seek a career after sport. I obtained a professional teaching qualification and used my degree to join the police force. I had a 30-year career, finishing as a detective inspector.

To the casual observer, signing the Chesterfield-born Miller was an obvious thing to do, but it very nearly didn't happen, according to Edwin.

Denis Smith didn't rate Geoff when he was coach and saw him in the nets. He wasn't going to sign him, but I told him that I thought he could make it and pushed Geoff's case. Mind you, I thought he would become a batsman who bowled a bit, whereas his stronger suit became his bowling. It took him much longer than it should have done to record a century and he never scored the runs that his talent suggested, but he was a very good cricketer.

Brian Bolus came in as captain for 1973. He had held that role at Nottinghamshire the previous year and was a sound, if cautious leader and solid, if not spectacular batsman. Derbyshire's East Midlands neighbours had finished only just above them in 1972, also winning one match, and a more innovative approach might have been beneficial. Edwin thought so.

Brian had scored a lot of runs with Yorkshire before moving to Nottinghamshire. He was past his prime, but had a good technique and gave important experience to the batting. Brian took the first team practice sessions and got a decent team spirit together, despite results, but what we needed at the club only arrived with Eddie Barlow a few years later.

The ill-fated 'Trueman experiment' was repeated with the signing of Clive Inman, for one-day cricket only, in 1973. The Ceylonese had been a prolific batsman for Leicestershire from 1961 to 1971, but had retired at the end of that season. After a season out of the first-class game, it was unrealistic to expect him to rediscover former glories and the move was another doomed to failure.

Young players continued to show promise in 1973, but the batting was erratic. Only Mike Page, who did so without scoring a century, and Brian Bolus passed a thousand runs, the others being some way off. While Hendrick matured quickly and led the attack well, he had little support, Alan Ward bowling only 100 overs during the summer. Venkat and Swarbrook formed a good spin combination, but they rarely had runs to bowl at and it proved a tough season. Only five John Player League matches were won, while the only Benson and Hedges Cup win was against the Minor Counties.

It could have been much better had Ward and Hendrick been able to bowl together.

> Alan was 25 and had only bowled 200 overs in two seasons. There was always something wrong with the lad, but I thought back to people like Les, Cliff and Harold, all of them willing to bowl even when they weren't fully fit. Alan wasn't. We had a few differences, some of it down to his attitude as he recovered from injury, but I actually felt sorry for him.

> In five years he had gone from being the most talked about bowler in the country, to nowhere. At the end of 1973, I wasn't sure where his career was going, to be honest.

Things had come to a head in June of that year, when Ward had been sent off the field by Brian Bolus, for refusing to bowl against Yorkshire. 'When Brian asked me to bowl, something exploded inside me. I couldn't go on .... I just wanted to get off the pitch,' said the player afterwards. He had taken the early wicket of Geoff Boycott, but John Hampshire, having been in discomfort against him before lunch, hit him for 31 from his next three overs and out of the attack.

After tea, when Bolus asked him to return at the pavilion end, he told him that he was unable to do so, having lost confidence after problems with his run up. After his captain left the field for discussions with the Derbyshire secretary, Major Douglas Carr, Bolus returned and made a dismissive gesture, the player walking off and leaving the ground before the close of play. The following day he apologised, but two days later announced his retirement from first-class cricket, his contract being cancelled by mutual consent. It all came as a shock to Edwin.

> I don't really know what happened. I was away with the second team and only heard about it later that evening. I think that everything just got on top of Alan. Maybe it could have been handled better and things do happen in the heat of the moment, but the bottom line is that you just don't refuse to bowl in a match. You get on with it and do your best.

To his credit, Ward returned and was back to something like his best in 1974, taking 56 wickets at just under 21 runs each. Hendrick was above him in the averages, but was away with England regularly and played only 12 Championship matches. It left seam support in the hands of the willing but considerably slower Keith Stevenson and Phil Russell.

Frustratingly, the spin attack had a bad year, Venkat's 31 wickets costing the same in runs, while Swarbrook had only 21 wickets at 55 each. At least Geoff Miller made progress, at the age of 21 taking 42 wickets and suggesting potential with the bat.

The batting should have been less of an issue, as West Indian star batsman Lawrence Rowe had been engaged to considerable fanfare. During the winter of 1973-74, before he arrived at the county, Rowe had scored 302 for the West Indies against England in Barbados. This had dispelled the idea that he could only make runs on his home wicket in Jamaica, while suggesting that Derbyshire supporters were in for a feast of runs from a batsman of charm and class.

It didn't work out that way. On his debut against Sussex, at a freezing County Ground, Rowe scored 38 in the first innings and 94 in the second, all of them while wearing pyjama bottoms under his cricket trousers, as well as every sweater he could lay his hands on. His square cutting was especially impressive, but it remained his highest score for the club. What went wrong? Edwin supplies the answer.

> He was a lovely lad, but he had such bad luck with injuries. He arrived with a niggle in his ankle, picked up a shoulder injury and had trouble with his eyes, a problem that was later to require surgery. Then we found out he had an allergy to grass and the story quickly went around that if Lawrence was sniffing, put Derbyshire in to bat!

> His problems meant he didn't practice as much as he should have and he kept making beautiful thirties and forties, then finding a way to get out. At times he looked so composed, so balanced and had so much time to play the ball that you wondered how he did it.

> His playing peak didn't last all that long and it didn't work out for him or us, but he was a lovely, laid-back lad and a very elegant player. With better luck he could have been one of the all-time greats.

Derbyshire won that opening game of 1974 but were to win no more Championship matches that summer. Two wins in the Benson and Hedges Cup was an improvement, but they still didn't progress from the group stage, while a first round defeat against Hampshire in the Gillette Cup at Derby was inevitable, once the home side had been bowled out for just 86.

The John Player League saw only four wins and a third-bottom finish. Rowe's 72 against Worcestershire at Ilkeston was the highest individual score by a Derbyshire batsman in the competition and indicative of the main problem. The side simply could not score enough runs and Rowe, who just scraped past a thousand in the County Championship, was the only one who did.

It would be easy, not knowing the way the club was run, to lay the blame at

In the nets.

Eyes on the ball.

the door of the coach, but people were generally understanding, as Edwin explains.

> Brian Bolus was some way off his best, as was Mike Page. Alan Hill came in and showed great promise, but he was a young lad and couldn't be expected to carry the side. We hadn't the experience for big scores, nor for bowling sides out.

> Losing Mike to England was great for him, but a blow for us, while Venkat wasn't close to his best either. It amounted to a very frustrating summer.

As the end of the season approached, Edwin received a letter from the club, saying that they would be dispensing with his services at the end of the season. The financial situation had become so precarious that two young players of potential, Colin Tunnicliffe and Bob Swindell, were released, while the club dispensed with its second team and gave up on Club and Ground matches, the usual conduit into the club for young players. Tunnicliffe was later to return and become a fine bowler for the county, but the club was in turmoil.

An approach was made to Derby Borough Council to take over maintenance of the County Ground, a potential saving of £6500. They refused, offering £100 per day of cricket, or £1200 in 1975, but it was not enough. While the club offices remained at the ground, their continued existence, at least in the short term, became a nomadic one.

In his annual report, the club chairman, Ken Turner, made the club's parlous state quite clear. He said that the immediate aims were only survival, and a return to the club's successful playing days of a few years before. They made for an unlikely pairing, the latter dependent on resources that the club simply did not have.

Edwin never had a contract, merely a gentleman's agreement.

> I didn't get a big lump sum. I got £100 and a thank you for my services. After all those years I think they saw me as a stick of furniture, nothing more. When that sort of thing happens, you start to think back over silly things, like when we were short of bath towels and Jean and I went and bought some ourselves from a shop in Sheffield. Or how we never got paid for cleaning the indoor school.

> Fred Swarbrook took a collection from a few of the younger lads and they gave me 200 cigarettes, but that was it. Twenty-four years and gone, like that. It was difficult not to feel bitter.

Derbyshire were unable to afford another coach until 1976.

Chapter Twenty

The retired cricketer

Edwin had an early opportunity to get back into the game and go onto the first-class umpires list, but he turned it down.

> I had 24 years of travelling the country all summer, but seeing very little of Jean and the children. It is a difficult life for any woman left at home, bringing up the family and effectively running the house. It wouldn't have been fair on any of them if I had then committed the rest of my working life to doing exactly the same.

Instead he went back to Grassmoor and into a full-time job with the Coal Board that winter. He worked in the stores at Duckmanton for three years, before moving to the engineering workshops, where he built pumps until 1987. Then, like so many others from a mining background across the country, he was made redundant.

Finishing work at the age of 52 hit the family hard. The work simply wasn't out there and the family stayed afloat thanks to Jean's earnings as a school dinner lady, once the children were old enough to enable her to go back to work.

> Nowadays the Professional Cricketers Association is there to help out in times of hardship, but we got no help at all. What savings we had went to keep us afloat during the year-long miners' strike. We just learned, like many other people, to cut our cloth to suit and did without things that we regarded as non-essentials.

> Thankfully we had paid off our mortgage by that stage and we managed to make ends meet. When we moved back to Grassmoor from Ashgate in 1998, we managed to make a fair profit in down-sizing, which has left us comfortable since.

He continued to play cricket long into retirement from the first-class game, first in the Yorkshire Council League, where he took 99 wickets at just six runs each for Norton Oaks in his first season after he left Derbyshire. He was professional there for three years and later played for Derbyshire over-50s. He played in their national County Championship triumph of 1992, before finishing in regular cricket at Chesterfield.

There were also regular appearances for representative sides of the Yorkshire Council League and the Bassetlaw League, where his skills and ability continued to make him a feared and respected opponent.

He continued to coach in Chesterfield until just short of his 80th birthday. He remained a popular figure and commanded respect from adults and

Assorted cricket trophies.

Chesterfield Cricket Club – Derbyshire Cup winners.

juniors alike, all of them aware of his record in the first-class game. What did he say to young spinners?

> I told them to work hard and to keep bowling until they could put the ball where they wanted it to go every time. *Then* work on spinning it different amounts. Get used to bowling just outside off stump, so their natural break will hit them, but cultivate an arm ball that keeps going away from the batsman and keeps him on his toes. It's not easy, but it will come if an individual is prepared to work at it enough.

It is sad when former champions are allowed to fade away, without their experience and talent being utilised, even on an occasional basis. Had any Derbyshire spinners over the years ever sought his counsel?

> No, and I find that quite sad. The only Derbyshire spinner who ever asked me questions and for help was Greg Smith, before he went to Essex. He asked me to show him how I bowled and then worked on spinning it more himself. Most of them today just roll the ball across their fingers, they don't 'tweak' it like we used to do.

> In recent years Derbyshire have sent lads to India and spin bowling clinics at great expense – I'd have been happy to work with them and give advice and they would only have had to come to Chesterfield!

Edwin and Jean now live in comfortable retirement in the Grassmoor village where they both grew up. Their oldest daughter, Diane, worked for Derbyshire County Council, but suffered ill-health and sadly passed away in 2006, aged only 45, leaving two sons, Mark and Christopher. They live at Matlock.

Younger daughter Fay lives in Shardlow, near Derby and is a solicitor, married to Mark Williams, a partner in the same legal firm. Their son, Ben, is at school at Trent College, Long Eaton and plays cricket for South Derbyshire under-13s, as well as hockey for Nottinghamshire under-14s.

Ask him about his time in the game and his eyes light up, the stories coming one after another. Who were the best batsmen he bowled to?

> One who stands out was Keith Fletcher. He was a wonderful player of spin bowling, but both Doug Insole and Trevor Bailey at Essex made you really work for wickets. All of them gave spin bowlers headaches.

> Peter May was equally at home against pace and spin and loved to dominate. There were two left-handers too – Peter and Dick Richardson at Worcestershire – who played off spin very well. They both took good strides and swept or lapped against the spin, both of them were hard to bowl at and were fine players.

> Harry Pilling was another. He was small and bowling conventional lengths was no use against him. You had to find different ones, or he would be quick to drive you, or, if you dropped short, he was a terrific cutter and puller.

As for spin bowlers, he willingly proclaims Shane Warne perhaps the

Derbyshire Over 50s XI.

Edwin and Jean in retirement.

best he has seen, while being less convinced in the legitimacy of Muttiah Muralitharan's action.

When I watched Muralitharan, I thought back to the treatment Harold Rhodes had and it saddened me. Bruce Dooland and Richie Benaud were wonderful leg spinners, while George Tribe was also an outstanding bowler.

In the 1950s and 1960s, there were probably a dozen off spinners who never got an opportunity in international cricket, all of them much better than the best of the current batch. It was a different world.

Edwin still follows cricket and the fortunes of his beloved Derbyshire.

Old habits die hard.

Chapter Twenty One
Master on the baize

Despite a 20-year playing association with Derbyshire County Cricket Club, followed by three more as coach, this is dwarfed by Edwin's snooker career, that started in 1948, when he was able to join the Grassmoor Snooker Club.

That association has continued for 66 unbroken years; he has won most trophies that have been worth winning. When I asked to see his trophies he laughed and told me that he would look 'some' out for my next visit, the following day.

I walked in to a room where the table was laden with impressive trophies, boxes with more in them on the floor to the side. The anecdotes were soon flying.

> I remember when I played Cliff Thorburn. He had just won the World Masters and I got to play him because I had won a competition to mark the centenary of the Derbyshire National Union of Miners. The final was played at the old Ashgate Drill Hall, where they got a table in especially for the event. I played a chap from Shirebrook in the final and beat him, four frames to one, winning a week's holiday at the miners' holiday camp in Skegness for my family.

> Well, Mike Watterson, who started the Embassy World Masters at the Crucible, in Sheffield, got Cliff to come through for an exhibition match against me, as another part of the prize. I had played Mike a few times at Grassmoor and he had won the National Club and Institute All England Snooker Competition, but I used to beat him.

> When the professionals played these exhibition games on promotional tours, it was traditional to give the local man a 25-point start. Mike told Cliff that if he gave me a start, I would beat him! So we played on a level basis and he won – but only narrowly, so I guess Mike was right ...

It is little more than one would expect from a man with a record break of 130. The stories come thick and fast.

> Mike and I played in a pairs competition at Cannock and had we won we would have been in a televised competition. We lost in the end, but one of the chaps we played against asked me why I wasn't playing as a professional.

> The answer was simple. I was playing cricket in the summer at the time when I was really good and snooker was very much a closed shop in the 1950s and 1960s, when Fred and Joe Davis carried all before them.

Edwin started playing snooker on a small table at home when he was eight and joined the local snooker club as soon as he was old enough, at 14. There were seven tables and he played regularly, soon getting good enough to beat older, more experienced players.

I played my first match against Wally Baker, who was then secretary of the Chesterfield and District League. I played at the village snooker hall until I was 18 and then was made a member of the Grassmoor Working Men's Club in 1952 and I have been there ever since.

We have been in division one of the Chesterfield and District League all that time, which is quite an achievement. I've won the individual competition twice and the pairs competition four years running, as well as winning every other competition that they put together at least once.

Among many trophies, Edwin is proud of his two wins in the Grand Masters, a competition for over-55s, but he has wonderful memories of games against some of the biggest names of the sport.

We used to go to Pontins on holiday when the children were young and I won tournaments there. I played John Spencer at Morecambe one year, after winning a competition there and played David Taylor, 'The Silver Fox', at Brixham, after winning that one. These wins were nice, because you then got free accommodation at the national finals, which were held in September at Great Yarmouth. It was good to get a few days away at someone else's expense!

I played against Ray Reardon when he was an amateur. He turned out for Cheadle and then I played him when he turned professional in an exhibition match at Spondon, for Bob Taylor's benefit. Ray Edmonds, who used to commentate on the snooker, was someone I played a few times, as he turned out for Skegness, while I also played against Nigel Bond a few times.

What about professional cricketers? Were there any good players among them?

Alan Revill was perhaps the best of the Derbyshire players in my time, but he wasn't good enough to have played at league level. A few of the rest played, but weren't especially good at it. I remember playing Mike Page one time and he couldn't figure out how I kept leaving myself on the black, after a red!

Two of the better ones were Brian Close and Fred Trueman at Yorkshire. One year we were playing them at Chesterfield and the landlord of the Boythorpe Hotel, round the corner from Queens Park, asked me if I could get Fred to go along and draw the raffle they were having for the old folks.

Fred agreed to go round on the Monday night and I said I would meet him there around ten to nine. I got held up in traffic and it was around quarter past nine when I got there. There was no sign of Fred, so I went

Snooker medal – highest break 1995-96.

Snooker trophies.

up and asked the landlord if he'd been. He raised his eyebrows.

'Has he been? He's played two blokes in there for a pound a game, won them both, drawn the raffle and gone!'

Asked if he ever considered turning professional, Edwin answers quickly.

No. I was a good player, but to turn professional I would have had to play and practice all year round. The demands of professional cricket meant I couldn't do that in the summer, so I was content with playing as I did.

My best years at snooker coincided with my playing career and to get on to the professional circuit I would have needed a sponsor, something that was harder to get then than now.

I've had a lot of good times at it though!

Chapter Twenty Two

Team mates and friends

When assessing the merits of someone, the best insights come from speaking to their contemporaries. While allowing for looking at the past through rose-tinted spectacles, the consensus of team mates and opponents was that Edwin was a very good and extremely unlucky cricketer.

Take the comments of Mike Page, an acknowledged fine player of spin bowling, who played alongside Edwin between 1964 and 1971 and for Derbyshire until 1975.

> I played with Edwin and also with Venkat in his time at the club. Venkat was a lovely guy, who came with a big reputation, having taken over 150 wickets in Test cricket as part of their classic quartet alongside Prasanna, Chandrasekhar and Bedi. I roomed with him regularly when we went to away games and got to know him really well.

> To be honest, on English wickets, I would take Edwin first, every time. You could get down the wicket to Venkat, use your feet and work it around. He was used to flighting it more and had a lovely loop – but it was much harder to get after Edwin. He would do you in the flight, could turn it different amounts and had this fantastic arm ball, that you always had to watch for.

What about as coach?

> He was shrewd, very quick at seeing flaws that creep into your game and helping you to adjust. He was especially good with young players and he helped the younger ones to build the techniques that later stood them in good stead in the county game.

Now 87, Barbados-born Laurie Johnson played cricket alongside Edwin for much of his first-class career and scored over 14,000 runs in entertaining style. He is well placed to comment on his former team mate

> Edwin was a fine bowler – you don't play cricket at that level for two decades without being very good at your job. I think he could have been even better, but for much of his career he bowled to his captain's instructions to keep it tight. Most of the time he had to keep an end secure while the seamers worked away at the other and someone had a breather.

> If I cast my mind back, I don't recall many days when he wasn't on the spot and doing exactly as he was asked. He was respected by all of us who played with him and by the teams that we played.

He was a consummate professional and can be proud of that last word, because it summed him up in everything that he did. Whether in practice, matches, his appearance or his attitude, Edwin was an outstanding professional, thorough and committed in everything he did.

Peter Gibbs is another who remembers Edwin well. He played for Derbyshire between 1964 and 1972, scoring just under 9,000 first-class runs in an attractive style, before retiring to become a successful playwright, script writer and author.

When I think of Edwin it is with words like stoic, stalwart, patient, tolerant and affable. To be a reliable professional for the length of time that he played is quite a feat. I know as a coach that he was able to bowl a tight line and length well into his seventies and that's a sound attribute for instructing younger players. He was a good timer of a ball too, especially strong square on the off side.

He was a particularly good bowler on flatter wickets, where patient application was called for. I remember him bowling Colin Cowdrey at Burton-on-Trent, much to the batsman's dismay, since he wanted a bit of pre-Test match practice on a decent batting track!

Brian Jackson is another who speaks of him highly.

Edwin was the best! I loved the guy and he was so reliable – if he got hit occasionally you put it down to a batsman's good day, because he seldom had bad ones. I will always remember that perfect arm ball he bowled to Basil d'Oliveira at Kidderminster, but you always knew that he would be probing away and testing the batsmen.

If he played today, he would walk into the England side. There's no one in the same league as him in the modern county game.

What has Walter Goodyear, groundsman at Derby throughout Edwin's career, to say?

As a player and as a man, he was one of the best. You would struggle to find anyone with a bad word to say about him. His wife and mine were very good friends and I came to know Edwin well, both professionally and socially. He'd have liked a bit more turn on my wickets at Derby, but he never complained, he just got on with it.

Yorkshire and England legend Geoffrey Boycott was typically succinct and to the point when asked for his thoughts on Edwin.

Nice man, lovely off spinner, caught me at backward point, diving left-handed when I was on 99 .... Bastard!

Praise also came from an unexpected quarter, when the name of Edwin Smith featured in a best-selling novel by top crime writer Martin Edwards, who explains that the inspiration was the Derbyshire spinner.

Edwin Smith was one of my favourite Derbyshire cricketers when I was growing up, and his name, along with the names of many other Derbyshire cricketers, past and present, features in one of my detective novels.

When I was working on my first book, I had to figure out what names to give to my fictional characters. The names needed to suit the storyline and be credible, and preferably a little unusual, but as a lawyer, I was conscious of the need to avoid libel. It seemed to me that an entertaining solution was to take surnames from players in my favourite football and cricket teams, people who could not possibly be confused with the characters in my murder mysteries.

My first book used several names from Derbyshire teams over the years, and this became a recurrent in-joke. It's a light-hearted way of expressing my lifelong enthusiasm for Derbyshire cricket and my genuine admiration for the people who play for the club.

David Steele was a Northamptonshire stalwart for many years, before becoming a national hero for the way that he stood up to the Australian pace barrage in 1975, then the West Indies in 1976. He later played for Derbyshire between 1979 and 1981, captaining the side in his first season. He remembers Edwin well.

He was a terrific bowler, one who always needed treating with the utmost respect. He rarely bowled a loose delivery and he had this terrific loop that made picking the length problematic. Then there was his arm ball, which caught out many unsuspecting batsmen, perhaps unaware that a spinner could swing a ball that much!

I fielded short leg in an era when we were expected to be right on top of the batsmen. Brian Close used to field on the edge of the cut strip and worked on the basis that if the ball hit him, someone would catch the rebound! Doing that, you had to have a lot of confidence in the bowler that you weren't going to be in the firing line, especially at backward short leg, which was my specialist position.

I would have happily fielded there any time for Edwin, because he had complete control of a cricket ball. He was a lovely man too, with a ready laugh and a smile never far from his face.

In short, he was a very fine cricketer.

Peter Eyre was a good county all-rounder whose career was sadly blighted by injury and ill-health. With better luck he could have gone much further in the game but remembers his time in the first-class game with fondness, speaking highly of Edwin.

There couldn't be a nicer man anywhere than Edwin Smith. I don't think he had an enemy in the world and he was always happy to help me whenever I asked for it.

Was he quite up to the standard of some of his contemporaries? Maybe not, but that was largely because he played on far less favourable wickets and there wasn't that much in it. He learned to bowl on tracks

Back at Grassmoor, October 2014.

On the attack.

that offered him little help and was a much better bowler on a good wicket than he was on one that helped him. That required bowling a different length and Edwin lost little in comparison to others of his time on a wicket that required discipline.

The subtlety of his arm ball stays with me, swinging away and sometimes going off the seam. He had a job to do in the side, in shutting one end up and he did that to perfection for over 20 years.

He should have played more one-day cricket than he did. We got a bit seamer-mad in the 1960s and Edwin would have given us variation, as well as being able to put bat to ball in the closing overs.

Colin Tunnicliffe was spotted and signed to the Derbyshire staff by Edwin and went on to take over 500 wickets for the county, playing a starring role in the National Westminster Bank Trophy win at Lord's in 1981. His memory of Edwin is of a coach who played a key role in the formative stage of his career.

When you are a young player you have all sorts of people giving you advice, but Edwin was a man who had a lot of common sense. He commanded respect, not because he imposed rigorous discipline, but because he was so obviously in command of and knew so much about the game.

I thought I was a decent bowler, but I had never seen a ball swing as much as Edwin's arm ball did and that was off half a dozen paces! He was a lovely man and always had time to listen to you and help. I will always remember him for the way that he made me feel welcome, when I first joined the club.

David Smith was a very solid, well-organised opening batsman who played with Edwin for several seasons, before retiring prematurely to take up a position in business.

When I joined the staff in the mid 1960s, Edwin had been a fixture in the side for many years and was always the under card to the fine seam bowlers that dominated the county bowling from season to season.

How talented was he? Well, he was a genuine finger spinner in the true sense of the word and bowled with a straight arm. He was beautifully positioned at the crease with a classic action and had the ability to bowl a very well disguised arm ball that fooled a lot of batsmen and collected him a lot of wickets.

I think Edwin was respected by all of our opponents, but the fact that he bowled mainly on seaming tracks meant that he would not be classed with the likes of Laker, Titmus and Illingworth, nor the two Gloucestershire spinners Allen and Mortimore.

Having said that, I had the pleasure of fielding first slip to him continuously for four seasons, so had the best possible view of his considerable talents.

Phil Russell broke into the Derbyshire side as Edwin was coming to the end of his playing career and went on to take over 500 wickets in all competitions, before himself becoming Derbyshire coach. He later moved to South Africa, where his reputation as a coach was cemented by much success. He is ideally placed to assess Edwin as a player and coach.

As a team mate he was always polite and helpful to the younger players. In those days some senior players around the circuit didn't offer too much advice to the new boys, because they were understandably protecting their own places. Edwin, like a few others at Derbyshire, was more accommodating.

For me, Edwin fell short of the very best off spinners of the era, who were Fred Titmus, Ray Illingworth and David Allen, because he played largely on seaming wickets and had less experience of and exposure to those that helped spinners.

He was a fine bowler, although Venkat was for me a world-class bowler who it was a pleasure to watch and learn from.

It is also worthwhile to take a view from a fellow spinner, Fred Swarbrook. Another who took over 500 wickets for the county, he came into the side at the age of 16 and bowled at the opposite end to Edwin for several seasons. Like Phil Russell, much of his later career was spent in South Africa, where he also became a respected coach.

Edwin was a superb team mate, on and off the field. He always made me feel welcome when I first joined the staff and he was happy to talk to me about bowling whenever he was able to do so.

Bowling on green tops didn't help him all that much but he fulfilled his role in propping up an end and keeping it tight while they had a breather admirably. While I wouldn't put him in the same bracket as the likes of Fred Titmus and Ray Illingworth, the bottom line is he took 1200 wickets in his career! In the many years that he played for Derbyshire there were plenty of spinners who were given trials and taken on to the staff and none of them were deemed good enough to take his place.

It is perhaps appropriate that the final word should go to England and Derbyshire legend Bob Taylor, who kept to Edwin for over ten years, as well as doing the same to Venkat and to Geoff Miller. He was better placed than most to assess and compare his talents.

Edwin was a very good off spinner at a time when English county cricket was awash with them. There have been times when a bowler of his quality would have found himself an automatic choice in the national side, because he was a very fine bowler.

I first met him when I trialled with Derbyshire and he had his arm in plaster. I saw him enjoying a cigarette that day and later, when I played with him for the first time, I saw his fingers were really badly stained with what I thought was nicotine. I was amazed that someone who smoked that much could be a professional sportsman, but it turned out that it was the Friar's Balsam that he used on his fingers!

He was a small man but had long fingers, which enabled him to really grip the ball and get good turn. As his career went on I think his fingers gave him problems and he bowled an increasing number of arm balls. I used to tell him to spin more and keep the arm ball as a surprise weapon, but that aside, he consistently took wickets to the end of his career.

Edwin gave no clue in his action that he was going to bowl the arm ball. I kept to John Emburey many times and told him that I noticed that he turned his head away when he bowled his version of it. He had no idea he did that and from the number of wickets he took with it, very few batsmen spotted it either!

Where Geoff and Venkat scored over Edwin was in their height. They were both tall men, as were his rivals over the years like David Allen, John Mortimore and Jim Laker. That gave them an extra weapon of bounce, which could be a potent one in the right conditions. Edwin was smaller, but without a doubt he was a very fine bowler over many years.

He's also worn very well and still has that quiff that makes him look younger than a lot of us!

The author and Edwin, October 2014.

Postscript

Edwin played his last cricket match in 2008, at the age of 74.

It was almost 60 years since he had first played for Grassmoor and his oldest grandson, Mark Burton, was captaining the Matlock Cricket Club Sunday side. They were short of players and Edwin was asked if he would consider turning out for them against Clowne.

He bowled ten overs and took three for nine, doing so well that he was asked to play for their second team the following week, in a league game against Darley Abbey.

He took five for 34.

Class, after all, is permanent.

Acknowledgements

I would like to thank all of Edwin's former team mates who are quoted in the book for their assistance and unfailing good humour in answering the many questions that I put to them in the course of my research.

I am especially indebted to Harold Rhodes, who was very helpful with general information and contacts, as well as to Peter Gibbs, who was both prompt and courteous in answering my requests for assistance in his role as secretary of the club's former players association.

Special mention should also go to David Smith, who made contact with Phil Russell and Fred Swarbrook when he was in South Africa and put them in touch with me.

I would also like to thank Geoffrey Boycott and David Steele for their valued insight of Edwin as an opponent, and the doyen of groundsmen, Walter Goodyear, for his insights into the period and the players. My time with him was both fascinating and memorable.

Thanks also to my good friend, crime writer Martin Edwards, for his support and encouragement since I started my blog on Derbyshire cricket (www.derbyshirecricket.blogspot.com) and for general advice on the writing process. Thanks to the Derby Telegraph for the historical photographs that I use with permission. Also to North Wingfield History Society for the photograph of East Street and to Grassmoor Cricket Club for their old team pictures. The contemporary photos of Edwin, his medals and trophies are by me.

I am also grateful to Mark Rowe of the Association of Cricket Statisticians and Historians, for keeping me on the right path as the book progressed and to the association for agreeing to publish it. Thanks too to proof-reader Kit Bartlett.

Most of all I would like to thank Edwin and Jean Smith. An interview for my blog made me realise that this was a story that was worth telling in greater detail. I am grateful for their hospitality, good humour and friendship. It really has been a pleasure to get to know you both.

Finally, I would like to thank my wife, Sylvia and children Stephen and Rachel. Their encouragement, forbearance and support meant more than I could ever say and I am glad to have you all in my life.

Bibliography

Regular Publications and Newspapers

Christian Science Chronicle, 1966; Daily Express; Daily Telegraph; Derbyshire County Cricket Club, *Yearbook* 1954 to 1975; *Derby Evening Telegraph; Derbyshire Times; News Chronicle; The Times; Wisden Cricketers' Almanack* 1951 to 1975.

Books

John Arlott, *Arlott on Cricket: His Writings on the Game.*
    Willow Books, 1984
Mike Carey (editor) *Edwin Smith Souvenir Testimonial Brochure.* 1966
Mike Carey, *Les Jackson: a Derbyshire Legend.* Tranters, 1997
Stephen Chalke, *Runs in the Memory.* Fairfield Books, 1997
Grassmoor Cricket Club, *Centenary Brochure.* 1984
John Shawcroft, *The History of Derbyshire County Cricket Club.*
    Christopher Helm, 1987
John Shawcroft, *Donald Carr: Derbyshire's Corinthian.*
    The Association of Cricket Statisticians and Historians, 2014
John Shawcoft, *The Harold Rhodes Affair,* Breedon Books 1987

Online

www.cricinfo.com and *www.cricketarchive.com*

Career Statistics

First-class batting by season

Year	M	I	NO	Runs	HS	Ave	50	Ct
1951	3	4	3	2	2	2	0	1
1952	12	15	9	37	11	6.16	0	6
1953	18	21	10	64	23*	5.81	0	1
1954	30	33	13	201	40*	10.05	0	8
1955	30	41	11	350	57	11.66	1	9
1956	33	45	9	440	41	12.22	0	17
1957	27	38	10	247	31*	8.82	0	10
1958	30	37	6	323	32*	10.41	0	16
1959	30	41	12	378	43	13.03	0	20
1960	11	18	4	204	22	14.57	1	6
1961	22	35	5	443	48	14.76	0	9
1962	25	33	8	575	90	23	2	5
1963	29	48	6	682	50	16.23	1	7
1964	29	44	5	722	58*	18.51	1	13
1965	30	46	3	423	33	9.83	0	23
1966	25	37	2	211	22	6.02	0	12
1967	31	40	5	552	63*	15.77	1	9
1968	27	32	7	483	50	19.32	1	15
1969	24	26	2	286	42	11.91	0	4
1970	24	28	10	303	28	16.83	0	10
1971	13	12	4	72	19*	9	0	4
Total	**503**	**674**	**144**	**6998**	**90**	**13.2**	**8**	**207**

Figures for 1955 and 1967 include one match in Scotland.

First-class bowling by season

Year	Balls	M	R	W	Best	Ave	5wi	10wm
1951	301	9	167	10	8/21	16.70	1	0
1952	1728	86	752	26	5/49	28.92	1	0
1953	2713	145	996	28	5/36	35.57	1	0
1954	3684	242	1446	71	6/60	20.36	4	0
1955	5270	320	1854	105	9/46	17.65	7	1
1956	4026	191	1804	60	7/58	30.06	2	1
1957	4528	247	1968	71	6/19	27.71	4	0
1958	3818	211	1521	54	6/70	28.16	2	0
1959	4463	196	2132	79	6/44	26.98	4	0
1960	1963	103	843	24	5/126	35.12	1	0
1961	3705	218	1482	46	5/41	32.21	2	0
1962	4015	283	1405	62	5/39	22.66	2	0
1963	3405	161	1636	38	4/64	43.05	0	0
1964	4194	232	1622	58	6/25	27.96	1	0
1965	4202	282	1412	71	5/23	19.88	1	0
1966	4821	320	1605	87	7/59	18.44	7	1
1967	5416	364	1927	84	5/57	22.94	1	0
1968	5484	352	2074	88	6/57	23.56	7	1

1969	3732	222	1538	51	5/73	30.15	1	0
1970	4765	246	2227	73	7/84	30.50	1	0
1971	2095	101	1037	31	5/64	33.45	1	0
Total	**78328**	**4531**	**31448**	**1217**	**9/46**	**25.84**	**51**	**4**

Figures for 1955 and 1967 include one game against Scotland.
Edwin's strike rate was a wicket every 64.36 balls bowled; his economy rate was 2.4 runs per over.

For comparison purposes:
Ray Illingworth took a wicket every 56.88 balls bowled at an economy rate of 2.13; Fred Titmus, every 61.28 balls, economy rate of 2.19; David Allen, 64.41 balls, economy rate of 2.2; John Mortimore, 62.75 balls, economy rate of 2.21; Brian Langford, 63.31 balls, economy rate of 2.34; Jim Laker, 52.14 balls, economy rate of 2.11; and Brian 'Bomber' Wells, 67.59 balls, economy rate of 2.15.

List A batting by season

Year	M	I	NO	R	HS	Ave	50	Ct
1963	2	2	0	30	28	15.00	0	1
1965	1	1	0	5	5	5.00	0	0
1969	2	2	1	29	21*	29.00	0	1
1970	2	2	1	13	13*	13	0	1
1971	1	1	0	12	12	12.00	0	1
Total	**8**	**8**	**2**	**89**	**28**	**14.83**	**0**	**4**

List A bowling by season

Year	Balls	M	Runs	W	Best	Ave	S/Rate	Econ
1963	165	7	106	2	1/46	53.00	82.50	3.85
1969	30	0	23	0				4.60
1970	58	1	35	0				3.62
Total	**253**	**8**	**164**	**2**	**1/46**	**82.00**	**126.50**	**3.88**

Index

A page number in bold indicates an illustration.